PLAY THE TAPE

5 SIMPLE WAYS TO STAY CLEAN AND SOBER ONE DAY AT A TIME

RECOVERY FROM THE ADDICTION OF DRUGS AND ALCOHOL IS POSSIBLE

BELLE MOTLEY

Dedicated to the addict who still suffers.

CONTENTS

**Go to www.bellemotley.com
scan the QR code for your free gift**

A Free Gift for You!

In the "Vibe Guide," you will learn...

- **15 techniques** to raise your vibrations and
stay in a high frequency

- How to manifest your desires

- How to find peace...

and so much more!

INTRODUCTION

One is too many, and a thousand is never enough. If this is a relatable statement, I guarantee that you're in the right place. That place is a simple guide to sobriety, the 12 steps, and handy information that has helped me and others obtain and maintain recovery from addiction.

Let's quickly get the cookie-cutter definitions out of the way. First, addiction is defined as a psychological or physiological need, which is often compulsive or chronic, for substances, activities, or behaviors. These behaviors, activities, or substances usually cause defined withdrawal symptoms when stopped. Recovery is defined as the process through which a disorder is combatted. Relapse is the recurrence of a disease or reversion into a previous state.

Take a breath after all that information and have a mint, candy, or piece of gum. This is especially handy if any part of those definitions caused a reaction. Notice how chewing that piece of gum or mint leads to a more relaxed state. This is not accidental.

What we've done by engaging our mouth is trick the primitive center of our brain into believing it's safe. That part of the brain is wired to believe that we have to be safe when we eat. Our ancestors weren't about to have dinner in the middle of a pack of wolves or alongside a crocodile. Instead, they sought out a protected area and then satisfied their need for sustenance. It's that hardwired concept we're born with that makes the gum chewing pause work to our benefit.

You might wonder what that cute trick has to do with the rest of the book. The answer is that it has to do with the brain, like an addiction. Addiction is psychological. It's a disease, a chronic illness, that affects the brain and changes the chemistry within the brain until it takes over and colors rational thought and reaction.

Can you be expected to take responsibility for a chronic illness? Let's think about this in terms of other such illnesses. I'm sure that you've found several references to mental health disorders in other reading materials, and there are obvious correlations between them. In fact, underlying mental health conditions are often a factor that plays into addiction. We'll discuss that in-depth later.

For the purpose of this segway, let's highlight another chronic disorder, Parkinson's disease, which is a degenerative muscle disorder that also affects neurological function. Basically, the pathways between the nerves and the brain break down and no longer interact the way they did before symptom onset. In this example, Parkinson's changes the way the brain interacts and reacts. It is a disease, and there is no known cure for it. What people diagnosed with diseases like Parkinson's do is manage their symptoms.

So, are you responsible for the disease of addiction? No more so than anyone afflicted with a similar type of mental illness or chronic disorder. The part of this that you are responsible for is recovery, which takes the place of management, and is really a more optimistic term. Recovery happens all the time from surgery and other illnesses. I mention it in that light because it then becomes an obtainable and sustainable goal rather than an abstract hope. Another thing that management and recovery have in common is they each take work, and they each come with a toolkit to make that work possible.

What you might wonder is why this disease affected you. Well, the jury's out for that one. As a general consensus, there are five different underlying factors that can make someone more predisposed to addiction. Actually, this list has some similarities to the underlying factors that cause diseases like Parkinson's or types of cancer. Genetics, environment, socioeconomics, personal trauma, and psychological disorders can each play a part in the development of addiction.

To put it another way, let's imagine that person we all know who's so fun at parties. She sips margaritas and sings karaoke or makes the entire bar laugh with her antics and humor. He goes to every house party and beach party, is captain of the football team or star athlete, and has such a good time that the entire crowd amps up with him. These are socially acceptable situations of substance use that may or may not lead to or indicate problems later. After all, no one's getting hurt, and everyone's having fun.

Until the margaritas at parties take the place of that morning's coffee, and the guy at the party is using his drug of choice to get through that 10 a.m. meeting and keep his amped-up state. Then, things start to change, self-talk echoes our fears and insecurities, and there's no way to even think about approaching that big task or next argument without a little help. The fun party trick becomes the tool that gets us from point A to point B, and our attention shifts from the way others feel to keeping ourselves steady, even, or numb. The ugly truth of the socially acceptable toolkit to fit in becomes a destructive spiral, and that is when we realize we have the disease of addiction.

The trouble with using only one kind of tool is that, eventually, it ends up doing more harm than good. That one-size-fits-all tool isn't as versatile as we might think. It becomes akin to a blender in a river. It's there, but it's no longer useful.

Like many chronic illnesses that addiction is compared to, there aren't definitive ways to determine who is more disposed yet. However, addiction research is an ongoing study, and understanding grows as more information is collected. Someday, there might be a way to offer better tools sooner.

For the present, getting clean and staying clean comes with its own types of toolkits. Think about the tools you use in the kitchen, the tools you use to fix things around the house, or the tools you use to complete chores or work. Each of those tools has a defined purpose and is built in a way that makes sense when used. Some of those tools can be moved from one kind of kit to another, and they do the same job. Others, like a spatula or juicer, are more specialized to achieve a specific outcome.

The sobriety toolkit is a similar idea. When you first decide that clean is the way to go, you might enter into a rehabilitation program. While in that program, the staff uses a specified set of tools to help you get clean and detoxify. That's step one, and there are tools in that kit that can carry over and be used afterward. For example, tools like journaling and affirmations are carryovers that help against the possibility of a relapse.

Playing the tape is my favorite way to stay clean. I play the tape when I feel like getting out of myself and getting into substance. What happens when I have a couple of drinks on a patio? I won't stop. I have never gone out and had a couple of drinks or a little this or that. It is game on when I get going and never ends well. Do I want to burn my bridges again and end up bankrupt, homeless, and broken? No!

I play the tape and go to a meeting, go for a walk, or call a friend. That doesn't mean looking back and feeling shame, guilt, and regret (you will learn to forgive yourself first.) It means don't forget that for us, one is too many, and a thousand is never enough. It can be really simple when we break it down, and that is what I am here to do. This is how I, and many others before me, have gotten and stayed clean and sober.

This book is for the addict prone to relapse, the people still in active addiction, and those new to recovery. Follow these steps, and you can do it too. You can be the best version of yourself. Remember, if you ever feel triggered, call someone, go to a meeting, or go for a walk, whatever you need to do to stay clean. You can do this. I believe in you.

1

HOW DID THIS HAPPEN (CAN IT GET BETTER?)

Remember that just because you hit bottom doesn't mean you have to stay there. The lesson is that you can still make mistakes and be forgiven.

— ROBERT DOWNEY JR.

L et's talk about rock bottom. You know that point where you look up and realize there's a wreck around you where life used to be? I got to this point because life got hard. I lived life, traveled, bought a home, had a car, a dog, and a good job. All of the activities in my life included social drinking.

And then life got difficult. I bit off more than I could chew and started drinking heavily—all day and all night. I became physically dependent and burned every bridge I had.

I ended up having a grand mal seizure, which led to my hospitalization. My liver and kidneys were failing, and I was given a 15% chance of survival. I had to learn to walk again, and they wouldn't let me leave without a plan. My story includes treatment, and that is where I learned the five steps.

There are many reasons we reach rock bottom, but the reasons don't matter. What matters is that you take the first step toward change. You can do it no matter how difficult it seems. It's just one day at a time.

ONE DAY AT A TIME

At the beginning of a 12 step program, we are handed a new kind of tool. It's a simple white key fob or a little card that's built to help us through the daily grind. It's a reminder that you're not being asked to stay clean for the rest of your life. Instead, you're being asked to stay clean for 24 hours one day, and on the next day, you set the same goal.

Let's talk about the one-day-at-a-time tool. You'll often hear it read aloud at 12 step meetings. There are a few variations to the wording, but each card includes similar ideas. This is a tool that's useful to guide your self-talk.

In Narcotics Anonymous (NA), new members are given a white key fob with "Just for Today" on the back. The front of the fob has the NA logo. The Just for Today message is read aloud at meetings. Taken from the Little White Booklet, Narcotics Anonymous (1986), this version reads:

- Just for today, my thoughts will be on my recovery, living and enjoying life without the use of drugs.
- Just for today, I will have faith in someone in NA who believes in me and wants to help me in my recovery.
- Just for today, I will have a program. I will try to follow it to the best of my ability.
- Just for today, through NA, I will try to get a better perspective on my life.
- Just for today, I will be unafraid. My thoughts will be on my new associations, people who are not using and who have found a new way of life. So long as I follow that way, I have nothing to fear.

Let's acknowledge how we address ourselves, that little voice in our heads that says, "Well done," or "You should've done that differently." These are examples of self-talk, which is how we talk to ourselves. Changing self-talk is a technique that helps us see ourselves in a more positive light and can help us deal with many types of stress. Guided self-talk, such as the card, helps us address ourselves without utilizing the negative tone we might have fallen into.

Does the idea of one day at a time mean that we forget about the future? Not totally, no. People, as a whole, have a tendency to worry about things that might never happen. For example, we act as though a tsunami in Kansas is entirely possible. Yet, the likelihood of a wave of any size rolling across hundreds of miles to the Midwest is nearly infinitesimal. What might actually happen is that the river that always floods will flood during the next rainstorm. We acknowledge that has occurred in the past, but let's not dwell on what the river's done or what it might do.

Instead, one day at a time means focusing on today's problems and letting tomorrow's problems happen tomorrow. What we can do is stow away a little for the rainy day to come, be it medical bills, retirement, or other future events that inevitably happen to everyone. The idea is not to let the coming rainy day take over every thought.

Having a one-day focus has a number of benefits built-in. First, there's the positive turn to self-talk. The steps outlined in the earlier card are actionable.

Next, we're setting a 24-hour expectation or goal for ourselves, which is a simpler achievement than the idea of sobriety for a year, five years, or longer. All of those are strings of 24-hour days stacked one after the other. Before you know it, you'll have reached a milestone, taking life and recovery one day at a time.

Another benefit of taking one day at a time is happiness. Moments of happiness might happen in the future, but we haven't reached them yet. The ones we noticed in the past and those that occur in the present are unique to those moments. To experience these moments of happiness, we must be present in the moment. If that flood or tsunami is all that you're planning for, those moments will happen without your notice. If we're living for today, we're there for the sunny days and the happiness ahead.

Now, I should point out that not every program subscribes to the idea of one day at a time. I point this out to emphasize that there are multiple types of programs, so if the one-day-at-a-time idea isn't featured in yours, it means that the program's toolkit uses different tools. The primary focus of this book is 12 step programs.

BASIC FACTS

I know that the very next thing you want to do is crunch some numbers. So I'll allow a moment for the groans that are sure to follow.

The fact is that addiction and recovery research has been and is still being conducted. There are numbers and percentages attached to recovery rates. One last fact, there are reasons that addiction is a chronic illness for some and not others. There are reasons Joe has Parkinson's and Bill doesn't or Sue has cancer and Mia doesn't. You can substitute any mental illness or other chronic condition for either of those examples.

So, let's discuss the numbers, and you might find these surprisingly interesting. The percentage of those with addiction who achieve and maintain recovery is probably something that's crossed your mind.

These conclusions were drawn in one eight-year study involving 1,200 people with drug addiction (Whitesands Treatment, 2017). About one-third of those who abstained from use for less than one year would remain clean. Of those that achieved one year of sobriety, less than half relapsed. Less than 15% of those who maintained sobriety for five years relapsed. Simply put, if 600 people reached a one-year and then a five-year goal, only about 90 of them relapsed. Even more simply, recovery is a proven possibility.

There are a few basic things about addiction that everyone should know. First, addiction doesn't care where you're from, what race, age, or gender you are. It doesn't care how educated you are. It doesn't care about your socioeconomics, although this can be a factor. If you're human, that's all it takes.

No one knows if a first drink or drug will lead them into addiction. Like any chronic illness, addiction is nothing to be ashamed of and isn't immoral. No matter how society may package its ideas on the topic, those close to us and those in recovery should understand that addiction is a disease. It requires treatment and counseling to reach recovery, even for those with the privilege and money to hide it. Treatment, as highlighted by the numbers, does work, and those who suffer from addiction can move on to live productively and happily.

The numbers are crunched. The basic facts are laid out. But, first, let's talk about the five factors which impact the likelihood of addiction.

Genetics

Bob has red hair. Mia is almost six feet tall. These two aspects of their appearance are products of their genetics. Genetics are the building blocks of how we look, inside and out, and these building blocks can affect how susceptible we are to certain diseases and disorders. It's the map of our makeup passed to us from our parents, who are also products of their genetic ancestry. Research into genetics is an ongoing process that frequently leads to a new understanding of how the human body and brain work.

There is also ongoing research into people who come from families with high addiction rates. Researchers have identified neural pathways, genes, and chromosomes as indicators of a higher likelihood of addiction. This type of research suggested a fifty-fifty relationship with environmental factors. This means that half the reason stems from genetics and half from their environment.

Recall how we tricked the primitive side of our brains through gum chewing and the hardwired response. Another hardwired response present throughout the animal kingdom is the pleasure and pain response. In general, our primitive brain seeks out pleasure and instructs us to avoid pain. Think of it as having another piece of cake versus not touching the hot burner.

When we do things that are pleasurable, our brains release a naturally occurring chemical called dopamine. Dopamine is present at varying levels in everyone's brain and can be triggered by several kinds of pleasure. For example, socializing, exercising, and other enjoyable activities can all elicit a dopamine response.

Some brains have a dopamine deficiency. Other mood-affecting chemicals, such as serotonin, can also factor into this, but dopamine is the pathway that has proven the most troublesome. In most studies (Murphy, n.d.), brains that lacked dopamine were more likely to form addictive pathways when presented with the usual suspects like drugs, alcohol, sex, and food.

These factors, researchers concluded, can create a predisposition to addiction. It doesn't mean that everyone with this predisposition will become addicted in the future. Similar things, like personality traits and brain structure, weigh in.

Others, like environment, early exposure, and individual choices, also play a role. What it does mean is that our genetics play a part, as they do in any chronic illness. Our genetics also have a role in recovery, whether with formal treatment or without.

Environment

Our environment is made up of all the people, places, and things we're exposed to day after day. The environment is defined not only as the conditions, objects, and circumstances we're in but also as the culture and society which impacts us. So, our environment is influenced by us but also shapes us.

Let's think about that river again. If we're standing on the banks of the river, it and everything around it is our environment. The river continues to roll down its course, seemingly unaware, but think about all the creatures that rely on the river both in and around it. Our presence might send fish into a scurry or make a woodland creature move downstream. Did you take a can of soda with you? If you leave it, that will have its own effect.

It's a pretty simple idea to believe the river affects us, right? A flood is hard to miss, and it might change the shape of the banks and cause damage to buildings, roads, and vehicles. To cross the river, someone had to build a bridge.

Our personal environment can be distinguished further through six general categories:

- **Family**. The risky types of families that may affect the likelihood of addiction are the types where there isn't an adult to look up to or if substance use is common.

- **School**. The quality of available friendships, a person's commitment to, and their performance in school can factor into addiction. These factors also carry over into the workplace for adults, particularly those in high-stress or high-demand work environments. Places where there's a need to decompress.
- **Peers**. The engagement and attitudes of close peers and a person's general peer group can be a factor. Inclusion in groups where a substance is regularly used can be a factor. Denial by peer groups can also factor, as substance use becomes a coping mechanism. Substance use in media that highlights the fun but not the consequences fall into this category.
- **Community**. If substance use and abuse are high in the area you live, the community is likely to factor into usage.
- **Trauma**. Sexual abuse, which occurs in childhood, has been linked to adult substance abuse. This can be a part of the family environment, but the lingering after-effects of several types of trauma often increase the risk of addiction.
- **Mental Illness**. Those who suffer from a mental illness, either diagnosed or undiagnosed, can use substances to self-medicate. This can quickly get out of control as it takes more substance to reach the preferred mindset.

In order to undertake recovery, there are a few parts of our environment that need attention. Lowering stress in our environment is one of these. This includes gaining distance from negative influences like friends still using substances. It also means our new environment shouldn't remind us of the one that triggered our substance addiction. It's up to us to make our needs clear to our support network.

Another thing that we'll need to do is avoid temptation and triggers. We should put ourselves around people who want to celebrate our recovery successes and stay away from those who can only focus on the negative. Also, the fewer substances around us, the more likely we are to avoid a relapse.

Finally, don't try to go it alone. Processing all the feelings that spawn from what happened can be a bumpy road for everyone. Instead, seek counseling to work through the feelings that led to addiction and those that emerge afterward. Joining a group like Alcoholics Anonymous (AA) or Narcotics Anonymous (NA) is another option through which we can express ourselves. The idea is to rebuild trust in ourselves and those around us and work through the hurt, anger, and other emotions tied to that time in our life.

Socioeconomics

We could crunch some more numbers here. Socioeconomics is another area where there's been quite a bit of research, and percentages abound from studies and corollary research. If it's so interesting, what is it?

Basically, socioeconomics is measured through a combination of income, occupation, and education. Think blue-collar and white-collar jobs or high school versus time spent in a trade school, college, or a university. The study of socioeconomics describes the amount of education pertaining to substance use, how substances like alcohol factor into social settings, and gives insight on how to focus treatment options. It's also commonly indicative of someone's overall quality of life, social standing and financial resources, health, and material wealth.

We'll skip the numbers and focus on the impact. It's a common misconception that the poorer someone is, the more substance use affects their lives. Substance use and addiction affect the rich and poor but happen differently because social norms are different.

Lower-income youth, for example, are more likely to binge drink. Meanwhile, those from middle-class households are more likely to sip drinks over an extended period of time. As a result, alcohol-related deaths are higher in lower-income households than in middle or higher-income families.

Opioids have a higher prevalence of dependency in lower income brackets. This may have to do with healthcare options as opioids are prescribed more often, longer, and in higher doses. This trend is further complicated by a lack of treatment options for people struggling with this substance at this income level.

Out of all the possible income levels, those who are homeless are presumed to have the highest addiction rates. However, research into this group is tough to substantiate because there's a high number of people who don't utilize shelters or outreach programs—basic survival needs and the lack of a consistent support system factor into these rates. Mental health also plays a role and can work against a person who is homeless and needs treatment.

It's important to mention that the Affordable Care Act has made treatment options more available. Many centers have sliding-scale payment plans. Those who are federally funded often accept state health insurance like Medicare, the Ministry of Mental Health and Addiction if in Canada, or you can speak to your local health authority.

Personal Trauma

We're going to get serious for a minute and discuss trauma. Trauma is a negative reaction to something that happens either in childhood or adulthood. The main causes of trauma can be physical or sexual assault, illness, accidents, natural disasters, bullying, parental neglect, emotional abuse, or domestic violence.

Adverse Childhood Experiences (ACE) are events in childhood that are traumatic. Those who've experienced ACE, such as household dysfunction, abuse, or neglect, may use substances as a coping tool, leading to addiction.

Enduring trauma can lead to post-traumatic stress disorder (PTSD). PTSD is described as an inability to recover from traumatic events. It's often characterized by surges of intense emotion. People with PTSD wrestle with troubling feelings and thoughts related to their past trauma. They might also experience nightmares, flashbacks, shameful feelings, fear, anger, sadness, difficulty staying in control of emotions, or isolation from others. PTSD lasts for an extended period of time, and coping with substances to feel better can lead to addiction.

In the case of physical trauma, there's a serious injury to the body. This can cause depression and a lack of confidence. Substance use becomes a tool to improve how we feel. In some instances, substance addiction leads to physical trauma if someone under the influence causes serious self-injury.

Emotional trauma may make us feel unsafe or hopeless due to bullying, humiliation, chronic abuse, discrimination, or a terrifying event. Substance use is a coping tool that can lead to addiction.

Treatment in the case of trauma is accomplished in several ways. If you have a dual diagnosis, such as childhood trauma and substance abuse, you may receive both medication and other treatments to handle both. Cognitive-behavioral therapy (CBT) may be utilized to learn new coping strategies and unlearn destructive thought patterns.

To help you heal from emotional trauma caused by a traumatic life experience, eye movement desensitization and reprocessing (EMDR) can be utilized. EMDR focuses on rapid and rhythmic eye movements.

Detox and inpatient treatment options are also utilized. Detox is when the physical system is cleared and "dried out" of all dangerous toxins. Detox should be undertaken with supervision in a medical facility to manage any withdrawal symptoms. Inpatient care is done in a facility and can include medically assisted detox, therapy, and counseling.

Psychological Dependence

I'm really craving that piece of cake right now. You know, the one from the dopamine discussion in the genetics section. If you missed it, there was cake, but maybe you were searching for the word "craving" instead. Well, here it is because craving has everything to do with dependence.

I will try to take the ambiguity out of the situation with a couple of quick definitions. Often, dependence and addiction are used interchangeably, but they are different from each other. These terms were so ambiguous that they were removed from the Diagnostic and Statistical Manual of Mental Disorders (Raypole, 2020) and replaced with the term "substance use disorder," which is measured from mild to severe.

Addiction is a chronic illness. Dependence is the process through which we grow to rely on a substance tool to feel a specific way. It's your dependence that leads to symptoms of withdrawal when you are no longer using that tool.

Let's move on to another type of ambiguity. There is a difference between physical and psychological dependence. Physical dependence isn't always bad. Think about Jack, who depends on his insulin to keep his diabetes in check, or May, who keeps her blood pressure down with pills. These are instances when depending on a substance benefits our health. What about your wake-up coffee? If you skip it, you'll have a caffeine headache because your body is physically dependent on caffeine. If you're physically dependent on your substance tool, you might have a reaction to being without it, such as seizures.

Psychological dependence is a whole other animal. This is when you feel you need something to get through a situation, handle certain things or feelings, sleep, or generally function. You have an emotional need for it, you can't focus enough to do something you enjoy without it, and you do it or think about it a lot. When you skip your coffee and miss it or even feel panicked without it, you're probably both physically and psychologically dependent on it. You crave it.

This means that when withdrawal happens, you can have two kinds. We're all familiar with the physical withdrawal symptoms. Post-acute withdrawal syndrome (PAWS) is a little less known. These symptoms include sleep problems like insomnia, issues with memory, concentration, disorientation, and making decisions, depression, anxiety, trouble with emotional control, apathy, difficulty with stress management, and personal relationship troubles. PAWS symptoms may last up to two years, depending on the length and severity of substance use.

How does all of that affect treatment? Well, for some, the psychological issues resolve on their own when the physical symptoms fade. But, for the rest of us, we'll need some help from a therapist. This type of therapy is about figuring out what triggers substance use and developing new behaviors and thought patterns.

THE DISEASE OF ADDICTION

In case you missed it thus far, addiction is a disease that is not your fault. I'm about to give you a powerful tool. It spans every kit and will probably carry over from a treatment facility or wherever your journey begins. We are powerless to prevent disease but can regain our power.

It's important to take responsibility for our recovery. If we own our recovery, we control where it goes. That doesn't sound earth-shattering, but it is a vital piece in our toolkit.

What makes taking responsibility for recovery so important? Well, according to AA's The Big Book, addiction is a three-part disease that affects our physical, mental, and spiritual well-being. The book differentiates these as a physical allergy, a mental obsession, and a spiritual malady. Let's break that down, and we'll circle back to responsibility with a little more clarity.

Firstly, a physical allergy is our body's reaction to the substance, which leads to craving more of it. Mental obsession is when the craving continues even after we've stopped using the substance. The spiritual malady is developed from our poor coping mechanisms, the traumas and injuries we've endured, and our personality traits. The spiritual list can only be understood through deep self-reflection.

Addiction is caused by a mash-up of circumstances, genetics, and other factors. Taking responsibility for our recovery gives us tools to combat it. The first step is admission. I admit that I am powerless over my addiction, and my life has become unmanageable. I admit that I am responsible for finding recovery. Then come the treatment steps, the meetings and groups, therapy, and counseling, which teach us tools and new coping strategies.

The second type of responsibility is commitment to recovery. It might be tough to fit in new strategies and ongoing treatments but think about the earlier list of things that factor into addiction. None of those happen quickly. So it stands to reason that recovering and learning new tools will take time.

We could reason that we aren't at fault, so recovery isn't our responsibility, but think about Joe with Parkinson's. He didn't ask for a degenerative disorder, for that misfire in his genetics, but he has it. At this point, Joe has two choices. First, ignore it and continue as is. The disease will only worsen without treatment, and now Joe's aware that it's there, which will affect his self-talk.

Joe's second choice is to seek treatment. With treatment, Joe's chance of living a longer life with slower onset of symptoms doubles. To keep this up, Joe has to take his medication, make all his check-ups, then manage any new developments. But, if Joe stays committed, he could enjoy seeing his kids graduate, get married, or meet his grandkids.

Taking responsibility for recovery becomes a tool that trickles over into every aspect of treatment and into life. It's an agreement with yourself to learn strategies to overcome cravings and use the one-day-at-a-time idea. It's an acknowledgment that you are willing to do the work and maintenance so you can be present and enjoy those happy moments that are sure to come.

The five steps, which we'll discuss a little later, is the treatment for our disease. When we work the steps, we take responsibility for our recovery. In case you wondered, recovery will lead to some changes.

WHAT WILL CHANGE?

Change makes anyone a little anxious. You might wonder if you'll become a different person or how you'll manage to socialize. Maybe you can't remember the last time you had a conversation sober.

Let me tell you, good things are on the horizon, and they'll surprise you. You will surprise you. You'll gain confidence and become more outgoing. You're going to make real friends. When you're sober, anything is possible.

Life Gets Good

What kinds of things can you look forward to? You'll be more in control and more in the moment. The moment, you know, when happiness happens. In case that's not enough, your coordination will improve. Your concentration gets better, and so do your alertness and motor skills. You're less likely to have accidents that cause injury.

Your organs will thank you. Your liver, brain, heart, kidneys, and others are all impacted by substance use. Every drink damages your liver. Cocaine is known to lead to heart problems. Each day that substance isn't introduced, your organs heal until they revert back to normal.

You'll have more energy and be able to exercise or do physical activity without feeling so drained. Your sleep patterns will improve, which means more rest. Your breathing will also improve.

There will be promotions in your future. Okay, if you want them, and this is because you'll be more focused at work. Collaboration with coworkers, attention to tasks, and the ability to meet deadlines are all easier when not under the effects of or thinking about substances. That job closer to home, with higher pay, or better benefits, is in reach thanks to your improved performance.

Your teeth, skin, and color will all improve. Weight maintenance may be easier as it stabilizes. You'll look as good as you feel and love as good as you look. Long-term substance use can impact a lot of different bodily functions. Physical factors such as poor blood flow, nerve damage, and emotional trauma can factor into arousal. You'll also be less likely to make choices that lead to sexually transmitted diseases.

People will want to be around you. When you started, you might've been the life of the party, but that ship sank a while ago. It gave way to the ocean of drama, lies, manipulation, and yelling that coincided with addiction. When substance use stops, you regain control and independence, take fewer risks, and save money. You also regain your pride, quality of life, dignity, and self-respect.

12 Promises

In case there wasn't enough of the good stuff earlier, an AA member from Ohio created a list of 12 rewards. This member presented this list at the International Convention held in Montreal back in 1985. Each reward links to each of the 12 promises, also called the Ninth Step Promises in The

Big Book. Here are the 12 promises as well as the coinciding rewards:

1. To know a new freedom and happiness. Reward: Hope replaces desperation.
2. Not to regret or shut the door on the past. Reward: Faith replaces despair.
3. To comprehend the word serenity. Reward: Courage replaces fear.
4. To know peace. Reward: Peace of mind replaces confusion.
5. To know that no matter how far down the scale, our experience benefits others. Reward: Self-respect replaces self-contempt.
6. The feelings of uselessness and self-pity disappear. Reward: Self-confidence replaces helplessness.
7. To lose interest in selfish pursuits and gain interest in our fellows. Reward: Respect for others replaces their pity and contempt.
8. That self-seeking will slip away. Reward: Clean conscience replaces guilt.
9. That our attitude and outlook on life will change. Reward: Real friendships replace loneliness.
10. The fear of people and economic insecurity leaves us. Reward: Clean life pattern replaces purposelessness.

11. To intuitively know how to handle baffling situations. Reward: Love and understanding replace doubts and fears.
12. To realize God is doing for us what we couldn't do for ourselves. Reward: Freedom replaces bondage.

Included in the promises for NA is the addendum that they have not seen anyone live the program relapse and the message that any addict can stop using their drug, lose the desire for it, and find a new way to live. Their message is the promise of freedom and hope.

Affirmations

- I surrender.
- I don't give up five minutes before the miracle.

2

WHERE TO BEGIN?

Sometimes you can only find Heaven by slowly backing away from Hell.

— CARRIE FISHER

That's a lot of positive change to look forward to. I'm sure your next question is, how do we start? I don't have a cute example or pithy story for this one. Step one is the same for the beginning of this journey as any other. Admit that you have a problem, open your door, step out, and get yourself to a 12 step meeting.

Using your preferred search engine, search 12 step meetings. Then tag the results near you, and you'll have a list of meetings, where they're held, and what times. There are online options for these, too.

Let's consider options for the journey into recovery. First, treatment and recovery feed into each other, but clinical treatment isn't necessarily the first step for everyone. In fact, treatment and the program can be viewed as autonomous paths to recovery.

Before delving into these options, a word on detox and its repercussions, many factors will affect this step into recovery. These may include medical conditions, age, gender, and the substance's length, frequency, and amounts. Detox generally takes between 3-14 days but can linger for several months. Severe withdrawal symptoms can be life-threatening. If you choose to self-manage this step, please seek medical attention if any detox symptoms grow extreme or life-threatening. In addition, you should have a complete physical before undertaking any kind of detox, supervised or otherwise, to ascertain underlying medical conditions that may have been caused by extended use or masked by your substance of choice.

In all honesty, the best option for you will probably have to do with several factors. However, I want to clarify that recovery is possible either way.

TREATMENT

Treatment programs that help rehabilitate those with addiction fall into two categories: The inpatient rehabilitation (rehab) facility, where you go and stay through treatment, and outpatient programs, where you live outside the rehab facility but go to it for treatment.

Consideration of a rehab facility can be broken down into the before, during, and after steps so you can evaluate the option with less anxiety. Two significant considerations will probably crowd your mind: Do you really need rehab, and how much does it cost? Since we're addressing these concerns as a consideration, let's begin with if you need rehab.

If you're considering treatment, then you're aware that substance is a problem and that addiction is a possibility. If you've acknowledged either or both of those, you've probably tried to cut back or quit using your substance. If you didn't succeed, then you know there's a problem underlying the substance use itself.

The longer you use a substance as a tool for whatever reason, the harder it is to stop. This is because we build a dependence on the substance. After months or years of reliance, our ability to choose erodes beneath the craving and influence of our disease. So, consider the length of time of your substance abuse as well as your frequency and amounts.

If you choose a rehab facility, the cost can be the next most daunting idea. But, did you know that most company, state, or provincial medical insurance will cover a healthy chunk of the cost of rehab? Facilities also have sliding scale payment options; there are may be some low-cost or free options and options through organizations like the Salvation Army or Catholic Church.

Keep in mind that an intensive, inpatient rehab facility will cost more than an outpatient program. The length of time spent in rehab, and the intensity of care required, factor into costs. The more severe your substance abuse, the more intensive methods are needed to help you with recovery.

Another thing that might factor into your choice is how you feel about treatment. Unfortunately, negativity and social stigma pervade the realm of those with addiction. This can be caused by our feelings of regret, shame, and guilt or by how our community perceives addiction—getting treatment sooner than later is always the right call.

Where to seek treatment is another consideration. Going out of state or province is an option and can help with your recovery for several reasons. Traveling for treatment can remove you from daily or local reminders and help you disconnect from work and family obligations so that your primary focus can be your recovery. Travel also widens your pool of available facilities. If you know you need to get away from where you are to focus on recovery, you should do it.

Once you've decided a facility is the right call, you can prepare to go by getting your life ready for it. First, if you have children, set up childcare with trusted family and friends who support your decision. Have a discussion with your children, especially teens, to mitigate any hurt or confusion that might result from your absence in honest, understandable terms about your decision and why it's important. Lastly, leave your shame and guilt with all the negativity and stigma outside. The more willing and open your heart and mind are, the more prepared you'll be to undertake the work of rehab and recovery.

Rehab will be different from what you're used to. Treatment lasts as long as it needs to, so there's no magic number for the length of time it'll take. Basically, the longer you spend on the first steps of your process, the more likely you are to have a lasting recovery.

The length of treatment varies depending on the person, and so the type of treatment will also vary. Another type of treatment that might be needed is medication. You'll undergo a comprehensive assessment to determine your needs when you start treatment. The treatment plan drawn up from this assessment will include any medications. These are most often administered during detox, for medical conditions, mental health issues, and severe opiate or alcohol substance abuse.

If you're given a dual diagnosis, your treatment plan will accommodate both diagnoses. For long-term substance use, a second mental health-related diagnosis isn't uncommon. For example, anxiety and depression disorders from chronic abuse are the most common. Other diagnoses, such as obsessive-compulsive or bipolar disorder, might require a more specialized approach.

The major difference you'll notice in rehab will be the schedule. The rehab day includes group meetings, therapy sessions, recreational activities, and free time. Alongside this schedule, the number of things you're allowed to have will be pretty basic. Everything you need will be in the welcome packet sent to you before you leave for rehab, and as long as you follow the packing list, you should be good.

Life after rehab will be different from the life you knew before. For some, the change from facility to regular life is a disorienting or overwhelming idea to process. However, life after rehab is about applying the skills and tools you learned to your new path and keeping a recovery mindset.

A great idea is to find a support group to supplement this mindset and make it a little easier to stay engaged in recovery. For example, you could find or even create a step group with your new circle. There are several kinds of support groups, so you can choose the type that best fits your preference and circumstance. In general, support groups range from men's or women's to substance-focused and Self-management and Recovery Training (SMART) groups.

Staying sober after rehab is a process that feeds into the program option. This process includes reaching out for help when you feel overwhelmed, working the steps through attendance and participation in support groups, and making choices with your recovery in mind.

However, if you should relapse, you have a couple of different options. For a short-term relapse, it's advised to bump up to daily meeting attendance for a few weeks. For longer-term relapse, returning to rehab is advised to get back on track.

PROGRAM

While we've all heard about rehab, that doesn't mean treatment is the only road to recovery. If the time spent in traditional rehab doesn't appeal due to being overwhelmed or lack of interest, there is another way. You can follow the five simple steps, which we'll cover in depth later.

The key takeaway is that a 12 step program is highly recommended to try during your search for freedom, no matter which path to recovery you choose to follow. This is because the program comes with its own toolkit that expands what you've already developed and provides instructions on how to use your new tools.

Join a program group that's right for you because it's vital to feel supported and surround yourself with people willing to help you get better. The common threads that link every member of the group create a web of support that is incomparable during your recovery journey.

WHAT IS A 12 STEP MEETING?

It's okay if you don't know what this is. I didn't know where to begin when I got to my first meeting. Twelve steps, is that a dance routine?

A 12 step meeting is a group of people all struggling to grasp a shared disease. You can expect to hear people recount what happened to them, how they're learning to take care of themselves, and what changes have developed since beginning their 12 step journey.

This is a meeting where you'll learn that you're not alone in your struggle and the benefits of having those around you that understand what you're going through. Members work through a 12 step process by beginning with step one and moving down the list in order. As members work the steps at their own pace, they begin to see a change from alienation to transformation.

Anyone affected by this disease is welcome at a meeting. It's entirely okay to sit and listen, to get your bearings, and to learn the process. There's no fee to attend. At some in-person meetings, a donation basket might be passed around to cover the rental of the space. The 12 step program and meetings are not a cult. It's a safe place for support and recovery.

THE RECOVERY VOCABULARY

When you sit in on a meeting, there are a few words that might come up you maybe haven't heard or that you recognize but not in the context they're used. Recovery has its own terminology. I'm about to give you "the list," and it will be yours to refer to anytime you need it. These terms can be descriptions of specific points in the recovery journey or terms given to tools used during recovery. Many of these terms will be expanded on as we continue.

Abstinence-based recovery: The strategy is based on complete and lasting termination of non-medical drugs or alcohol use.

Acts of self-care: Acts of responsibility undertaken to repair the damage done by addiction and establish healthier habits. This is not to be confused with self-centered acts while using or drinking.

Acts of service: Actions taken not for money or acknowledgment but to provide a real connection to others.

Alcoholics Anonymous: A worldwide, voluntary community of people from all backgrounds and experiences who come together in meetings to achieve and sustain sobriety.

Amends: The repayment of symbolic or literal debts or wounds amassed during addiction. Amends are personally given (unless doing so would hurt others) and is a pathway to potential forgiveness and atonement.

Anonymity: In a 12 step program, the principle of "who's seen and what's heard stays at the meeting" is upheld. This stems from the belief that the welfare and attraction of the meeting propel its members and not their personalities or names.

Cake: When someone "takes a cake," they are taking a year or more of clean time (one year, three years, etc.)

Chairperson: The person who leads the 12 step meeting.

Chips and medallions: Medallions or chips are used to mark abstinence in some programs. Each is etched with the amount of time sober and serves to reaffirm commitment to living a clean, sober life.

Clean Time: The time spent free of substance use.

Closed Meeting: Meetings that are limited to members and potential members.

Complacency: This happens when a person who has stopped using doesn't address the aspects that led them to their problem or recovery or stops actively working the steps.

Crosstalk: An interruption or direct response to another member's shared experience. 12 step meetings have a rule against this and advocate responding through personal narrative and identification. This rule ensures the continued safe space upheld in meeting rooms.

Defects of character: These are overly developed character traits that must be addressed to find relief from self-destructive patterns.

Deprivation: Not a part of the 12 step construct. Instead, the development of new attitudes, friends, and horizons is experienced through using social skills and coping mechanisms that are not possible while using a substance. Instead, 12 step programs stress freedom from addiction.

Disease concept: A concept that removes weakness from the narrative of physical addiction and, through decades of research, firmly sets it into the realm of a medical illness.

Drunkalogue: A share or monologue that glorifies past substance use experiences rather than following the share structure of "what it was like, hitting bottom and recovery, and how things have changed since recovery."

Faith-based recovery: These are alternative programs based upon a framework of religious concepts, experiences, and rituals.

Family disease: Addresses the concept of addiction as a family disease where facilities offer treatment for dysfunction, enabling, codependency, and other addictions within the family.

Family recovery: This is based on the concept of family disease. Research has shown that individual recovery should occur before family recovery. Family recovery includes heal ing, achieving healthy boundaries, and developing healthy systems within the family.

Fob: The key ring or token given to new members of NA. It begins as white, but as anniversaries of sobriety pass, new fobs are given to mark them.

Getting the Program: Grasping what the program is all about by listening to other members, experiencing the community, and gaining an understanding that by not engaging in addictive behavior, such as picking up that drug, you won't get loaded.

Give it away to keep it: The idea that by helping others suffering from addiction, you maintain what's been given to you during recovery.

God of our understanding: A concept that encompasses every person's understanding of a higher power and pointedly developed to move the addict away from self-will and into asking for help and developing a spiritual concept.

Gossip: In the 12 step community and programs, gossip is considered a corrosive habit since it can trigger others to use their substance.

Gratitude: To the recovering addict, this is the ability to be thankful for the good stuff in life and also a way to learn humility and willingness to give it away.

Higher power: A restorative power greater than oneself, defined as "God as we understood him" and meant to move you into a community and out of isolation.

Hitting bottom: The last phase experienced before recovery, which gives perspective and awareness that addiction has overtaken your life.

Homegroup: Finding a home group and regular meeting attendance are two recommendations 12 step programs make to those with addiction. A home group is their grounding group where others can get to know you, and absences can be noticed. It gives additional support during extreme life events to help against relapse.

Humility: In recovery, this aspect allows for change, admission of wrongdoing, personal responsibility, development of principles, and a healthy, honest life as a standard. It makes it possible to ask for help from the group, a higher power, a sponsor, or health care professionals as needed. On the other hand, being entirely self-reliant is ego driven and can be dangerous.

Intervention: This is a confrontation to help you admit your addiction and need for help, usually undertaken by your family, fellow addicts, or professionals.

Keeping it green: A strategy that reminds the recovering addict how quickly their progress and new life can be destroyed by substance use and revert back to how it was before recovery and reaping the benefits. It's a particularly useful tool for those in danger of forgetting who they were and where they've been.

Literature: A reference to the literature approved by the 12 step program fellowship and produced by the governing body. This doesn't mean other literature is bad; rather, there is some concept in the literature that the program can't put its name on.

Membership: 12 step programs require no fees or dues, but entry into the rooms indicates a search for sobriety and a better life.

Narcotics Anonymous (NA): An organization dedicated to the recovery of all those who abuse drugs, of which alcohol is one. It's an international organization that practices complete abstinence from all types of drugs and is dedicated to supporting those recovering so they can move into a life where they no longer want to use their substance.

Newcomer: A person trying to obtain sobriety and has recently started attending meetings. 12 step groups emphasize welcome and support for all newcomers. The newcomer is the most important person in the meeting because we can't keep what we have without giving it away.

90 meetings in 90 days: Based on suggestions from others in recovery, this is the idea that learning the program, listening in meetings, changing behavior, and learning how others share and manage their lives one day at a time are most beneficial to recovery over a 90-day period.

Normal drinker or "Normy": People who can order a drink, sip, and be finished. They are the opposite of those who've developed a dependence on alcohol, in which any drink leads to uncontrollable consumption.

Old-timer: A phrase that refers to those who've spent substantial periods sober and usually applies to people with 20, 25, or 30 years of sobriety. They're a reminder that a new way to live is possible without picking up the substance that led you into the 12 step program.

Open meeting: This type of meeting can be attended by anyone who wants to be there.

Powerlessness: The acceptance of the first step, which states we were powerless over (substance) and that our lives became unmanageable. Acceptance of this idea helps us develop an acceptance of the need for abstinence.

Prayer: A process that can take many forms and through which we communicate spiritually with a power greater than ourselves.

Primary purpose: To remain clean and sober and help others attain sobriety.

Principles: These are the concepts behind each step in the 12 step process. Some of these are hope, commitment, honesty, surrender, willingness, reflection, justice, brotherly love, humility, truth, perseverance, service, and spiritual awareness.

Program: An inclusive method to live with the principles of the 12 steps and use the support systems utilized in the rooms like attending meetings, sponsorship, using the slogans, and doing service.

Program of suggestions: A description of the 12 step program. There are no rules to the program. Instead, everything found in literature and the program are suggestions based upon thousands of narratives from others who've struggled to maintain sobriety and live a productive, honest, and healthy life. This is why self-exploration is so heavily advised, as one person's path may not entirely fit another's.

Promises: The promises listed earlier in the literature help those with addiction believe that working the steps and program can lead to freedom and happiness.

Qualifying: A story shared by a member which provides a unique opportunity to identify with the feelings behind the story of addiction and is framed in the share structure: how it was, what brought you to recovery, and how things are now.

Recovery: The path implied by working the steps and program walked by all those who've come before. It's a chance to regain your sense of self, rebuild relationships or make new ones, and learn to live in a life-affirming, healthy, and productive manner.

Recovery home: This is a communal living situation for those beginning recovery and is self-funded. Make sure it's a positive fit for you and your recovery.

Relapse: A time after getting clean when you return to substance use.

Reprieve: A break from the disease that underlies addictive behaviors and that every day is a fresh start.

Responsibility: The foundation for recovery where you are accountable for your past, present, and future actions, and blaming others for actions or decisions is no longer a reasonable excuse.

Service committees: 12 step members who help others in a specified room or in the organization by engaging in service activities.

Sharing: The discussion portion of the meeting, which is framed by the meeting topic. Through listening and sharing, we can identify with others' struggles and learn about our shared similarities within the addiction context.

Slip: A short time when substance use resumes. This term is for those who differentiate between a slip or relapse. They define relapse as a more extended period of use than a slip. Slips lead to relapse as it only takes one.

Sobriety or Clean date: Marks the sobriety date since last substance use. This date is used as a symbol of proof that the program works, and that personal growth and abstinence are possible.

Spiritual awakening: The process through which the recovering addict moves through self-reflection, admitting defects, and making amends which leads to experiencing new awareness of life, self, humility, or spiritual practice.

Spiritual health: The continuation of the spiritual awakening, which can give a sense of serenity, ease, or peace during a crisis and allows you to move through both joyous and difficult times in a healthy, affirming manner.

Sponsorship: Refers to the 12 step program's mentorship practice designed to help and strengthen both the newcomer and recovering member through a renewed connection to the rooms and helps overcome other emotions tied to recovery.

Step groups: Refer to the members of 12 step programs who are working on a specific step. Some groups have meetings specifically for each step.

Story: Pieces of our stories are shared in meetings where we share our experiences, strength, and hope. Longer stories are shared in speaker meetings, a deeper look into someone's journey.

Surrender: Unreserved acknowledgment that you have an addiction, need help, and that your willpower achieved nothing. Admission of powerlessness and the need for help is an act of strength.

Switching addictions: When you give up the addiction which drove you into recovery but transfer that behavior to another self-destructive or negative behavior. If the underlying reasons for your addiction haven't been addressed, you could lose your sense of balance, and your addiction can take another form.

Taking your will back: In line with complacency, taking your will back is when you begin to do the minimum and replace the idea of your higher power's will with yours.

Thirteenth stepping: This refers to a member with more sobriety time engaging with a new group member in a way that leads to sexual involvement. This is why it's advised for men to mentor men and women to mentor women.

Tolerance and open-mindedness: Bill Wilson established a belief that these two aspects were important to the long-term establishment of the 12 step program. This is why the AA or NA institutions do a close inventory and self-evaluation. This is also why the program acknowledges that sometimes help from a professional is needed since sometimes the program cannot provide everything you need to cope with life issues.

Tools: The term used to describe the methods utilized in sobriety. Things like sponsorship, steps, sharing, slogans, meetings, literature, and service are tools used to manage impermanent circumstances and emotions daily.

Traditions: The guiding principles of the functions of NA or AA, the meetings, and the organizations. These principles are based on the 12 traditions. In the Basic Text, Narcotics Anonymous (1986), the traditions are:

- Our common welfare should come first; personal recovery depends on NA unity.
- For our group purpose, there is but one ultimate authority—a loving God as He may express Himself in our group conscience. Our leaders are but trusted servants; they do not govern.
- The only requirement for membership is a desire to stop using.
- Each group should be autonomous except in matters affecting other groups or NA as a whole.
- Each group has but one primary purpose—to carry the message to the addict who still suffers.
- An NA group ought never endorse, finance, or lend the NA name to any related facility or outside enterprise, lest problems of money, property, or prestige divert us from our primary purpose.
- Every NA group ought to be fully self-supporting, declining outside contributions.
- Narcotics Anonymous should remain forever nonprofessional, but our service centers may employ special workers.

- NA, as such, ought never be organized, but we may create service boards or committees directly responsible to those they serve.
- Narcotics Anonymous has no opinion on outside issues; hence the NA name ought never be drawn into public controversy.
- Our public relations policy is based on attraction rather than promotion; we need always maintain personal anonymity at the level of press, radio, and films.
- Anonymity is the spiritual foundation of all our Traditions, ever reminding us to place principles before personalities.

Triggers: The emotions, issues, people, or places associated with your substance use. Navigating stressors or triggers is paramount to continued recovery, and chances for relapse increase if left unaddressed.

Trusted servants: The rotating positions of each group's steering committee. Since AA or NA as an organization is voluntary, these positions are also. The steering committee manages ongoing businesses, and positions can change every month, every three months or whatever length of time is determined by the group. The committee is made up of chairpersons who lead each meeting, secretaries who manage the literature and may hand out key fobs or chips in the meeting, treasurers who make donations or pay rent, and they can also have an intergroup representative. Each is a temporary position.

24-hour plan: This is the idea of maintaining sobriety in 24-hour, or shorter as needed, increments. Each day you say, "I will put using (my drug of choice) off until tomorrow," until the urge to do so eventually passes.

Unity: The common, unifying principle behind the goal of keeping those suffering from addiction sober. The program succeeds due to its unified purpose.

Willingness: This is the idea that in order to achieve the rewards of the program, a person must be willing to give up self-will and wholeheartedly seek change so that their life can become open to fulfillment. This idea includes being willing to ask for help, listening and learning, and seeking help from a greater power, along with other ideas set out in the 12 steps.

Working the Program: Utilizing and applying the 12 steps, traditions, and philosophies, being active in fellowship and embracing the program.

Working the steps: The suggestions at each step which is a comprehensive way to look at individual lives, past and present behavior and make a spiritual connection. Step groups are meetings that explore them in-depth, and each member tries exercises connected to the step under the guidance of a sponsor. Over the course of years, many members revisit or repeat the steps as their recovery phases lead to new perspectives and understanding, which allows for continued growth and change.

Affirmations

- I am finding freedom by following my program and having faith.
- I am becoming the best version of myself.

3

THE FIVE SIMPLE STEPS

*Little by little I found the beat again, and after that I found
the joy again. I came back to my family with gratitude, and
back to my work with relief.*

— STEVEN KING

Now we come to the five simple steps that can get you clean and help you stay sober. I'm sorry, but this isn't a dance routine, either. Instead, it's a recovery support toolkit expansion.

We're going to do this one step at a time, just like we'll take sobriety one day at a time. Before you know it, you'll have learned the five steps and be able to utilize them. Remind yourself of all the beautiful things that happen when you take responsibility for your recovery, things like happy moments and a you that looks and feels better.

MEETINGS

The 12 step program path has been laid out and successful for those before you. But, let's be honest; many fads are passing through the world, so what makes this program different?

AA was founded in 1935 by two friends struggling with alcohol use. It is the oldest of the 12 step programs and has the dubious honor of figuring out what works. NA was founded in 1953 by Jimmy Kinnon, who utilized the AA program structure as a model for a more inclusive fellowship for those struggling with drugs, including alcohol. As a need rose afterward, a new group was founded.

What is the structure of a meeting? We've discussed some of the things you might see and hear at your first one. Every meeting generally follows a similar structure. Meetings last around an hour, are held in rooms such as a church basement, a hall, hospital, or other rented space—they may also be outdoors—and are usually run by the members.

At the beginning of the meeting is a nonjudgmental welcome. This is an important facet to keep in mind. Everyone at the meeting is there because they share a struggle with addiction. Following the welcome, the 12 step traditions and literature are read. This is often followed by the serenity prayer.

"Grant me the serenity to accept the things I cannot change, the courage to change the things I can, and the wisdom to know the difference," is the short, most well-known version. Of course, there's a little more to it if the full prayer is recited, but this is one of those touchstones that will make you feel more confident about what's going on if you're new.

There might be related announcements made after the prayer and then an invitation to introduce yourself by your first name only. Introductions are voluntary, and after introductions, there could be a request for sponsors. In general, anyone at a meeting could be a potential sponsor, but each meeting runs a little differently in this respect. There could be raised hands for either sponsors or sponsees, a sign-up sheet, or a similar idea that works for that group.

At some point during the meeting is a celebration of sobriety, during which members announce how long they've been clean. This can be for those new or coming back to the program and 30 days or longer. You can expect applause, key fobs, and hugs as successes are celebrated. Once they've found their group, many in recovery come to view their 12 step fellowship like family.

After the celebration, people are asked to share experiences, thoughts, strengths, hopes, and what the program has done for them. They might read literature that has had a particular impact. Then they will open the discussion to the group on a particular topic, during which the group will share related anecdotes.

Other things likely to happen at any meeting include a collection basket passed around to cover things like rent, group materials, fees to national committees, or miscellaneous things like snacks and coffee. Second, there may be a request or invitation for anyone with a "burning desire" to share, which is an opportunity to gain the group's support in whatever area of your struggle might prey on you. A "burning desire" to share means that if the person doesn't share, they stand a high chance of using their drug of choice and might harm themselves or hurt others.

Part of the meeting is a moment of silence where members bow their heads for those suffering the most. This could be followed by a repetition of the serenity prayer.

Types of Meetings

AA and NA are easily the most well-known and recognizable of the 12 step programs. AA deals specifically with alcoholism and is likely to crop up in searches time and again. In addition, AA has a global community of members from all walks of life.

NA will be another program that comes up as often as AA. However, this program has a broader outlook and structure where you're as likely to find those whose drug of choice is alcohol as any other. NA isn't affiliated with AA or any other organization and welcomes anyone from any walk of life. They're interested in support and not in what you have or haven't done, who you might know, or where you're from. The NA program, also a global community, is one of complete abstinence from all drugs and welcomes the newcomer as the most important member of a meeting.

There are more programs available than AA and NA. They're grouped by type: substance, behavioral, and other. A search of 12 step programs and your substance or behavior in any search engine will offer up several options for you. For example, and this would fall into the behavioral category, there is an online gaming support program to help people struggling with gaming addiction.

Substance groups include AA, NA, Heroin Anonymous (HA), and many others. Al-Anon/Alateen is for friends and family of those struggling with alcohol addiction. Al-Anon is for adults and children. Alateen is specifically for teens whose lives have been affected by alcohol addiction.

In the behavioral category, you'll find groups such as Gamblers Anonymous (GA), Workaholics Anonymous (WA), or Overeaters Anonymous (OA). Emotions Anonymous (EA) is a support program for those struggling with emotional and mental illness.

In the "other" category are Celebrate and Refuge Recovery, which are faith-based programs, Wellbriety, the Native American program, SMART, and Mindful Moderation.

Zoom meetings are also available online. You can potentially find a meeting 24 hours a day, 7 days a week. Codes for 12 step Zoom meetings are available on the websites of any of the organizations.

If you can't find a group that you feel includes you, your substance, or your behavior, you can start your own. There are probably people like you who share the same struggles and wish they could find a group to offer and receive support.

SPONSOR

Sponsor is a word you're going to hear a lot as you undertake your recovery journey. A sponsor, in this sense, is a guide through the 12 step program. A sponsor helps you learn how to work the steps and discuss things that might trigger a relapse. They're a mentor who has been through the steps and the journey and has the experience you don't have yet.

As a general rule, sponsorship is a temporary gig. Keeping things temporary alleviates the pressure on both the sponsor and sponsee. That doesn't mean that you shouldn't invest in what your sponsor has to offer.

Remember in our discussion of meetings how people wrote their names down on a list or raised their hands? In some meetings, these are the sponsors willing to take on new sponsees. In alternative formats, it'll be anyone looking for sponsorship that's asked to raise their hands. In others, you can approach anyone present at the meeting. If you are unsure, I encourage you to ask anyone at a meeting where you can find a sponsor, and they will be happy to help.

Maybe you're nervous about this step. It's not always easy to build new relationships or face the idea of rejection because, yes, a sponsor can say no. You can mitigate this concern by listening to the shares and discussions of your group. Pay special attention to everyone that indicates they're willing to sponsor and even more attention to people whose stories resonate with you. It's a little like dating or finding new friends. They should be someone you click with and whose ideas mesh with yours. Program guidelines strongly suggest choosing a sponsor who's the same gender as you. Obvious reasons of possible attraction aside, which can make conversation awkward, this is all about life experiences and how they'll inform your sponsorship.

Let's be honest; a man's and a woman's worlds can be very different. The way that we support each other, the way that we think, and the way that we connect can be night and day different. This applies to the LGBTQ and nonbinary communities as well. You might think a same-gender sponsor is asking for trouble, but their path into recovery will still be more like yours than someone from the opposite gender, and that's what will be the most helpful in the long run. In smaller communities, it's entirely possible that finding a sponsor of the same gender proves a difficult task. Remember, this isn't a love connection, so choose the person whose story aligns most with yours. Look for someone who has what you want (not material)—it could be their family back in their lives, their children, a job, marriage, etc.

Once you've succeeded in finding a sponsor, the next step is using your sponsor effectively. You can expect a learning period that extends to both the sponsor and sponsee. Every sponsor approaches sponsorship a little differently. You and your new sponsor should do fine if you undertake the situation with willingness and an open mind.

Remember that a sponsor is a mentor or teacher, and everyone teaches differently. They might ask you to journal everything. They might ask you to set a goal for the day related to the step you're on. They might want you to call at a specified time every day. Our sponsor is aware of the pitfalls that might arise, and they're there to work with you to follow and apply the 12 steps.

Call your sponsor every day. This will help you pick up the phone when you need support. When you feel that some part of your life, be it medical, financial, or relationship, endangers your recovery, bring it up. Chances are, your sponsor has an idea or two about how to handle it. The longer your relationship with them lasts, the more likely they'll be to ask about personal things, but their focus should be on helping you through the 12 steps.

When you feel ready to move to the next step, bring it up with your sponsor. If they disagree that you haven't benefited from the step you're on as much as possible, continue to work on that step diligently and wholeheartedly. Remember that they have the experience that you don't.

If everything is going well in your life, it is okay to call and see how your sponsor is doing—they will appreciate it. The important part is you are still picking up the phone. Try to utilize this time and talk about any troubles, no matter how insignificant they seem to you. You have a sponsor to help you, so if you're in danger of slipping in the middle of the night, reach out to them. If you can't get a hold of them, try to reach someone else in your network. Preferably someone who can meet you face to face. Don't wait until after you've slipped to make that call. Your sponsor and network are there to help you maintain your sobriety.

Sponsors are as human as you are. There might come a time when you feel that you need to part ways with yours. We're not talking about after a disagreement when we make impulsive decisions based on bruised pride or hurt feelings. A sponsor's job isn't to be your cheerleader and agree with everything you say and do. It's their job to highlight the good and the bad, so you can see them, too. So, when a disagreement happens, take the time to cool down instead of rushing off to find someone else.

The time to part ways boils down to five straightforward circumstances, which we will explain shortly. First, sponsorship is considered temporary, but break-ups can still be tough. If you need to part ways, try to have another sponsor set up before this happens. Having a sponsor is important to your recovery, and recovery should always be your focus.

Trust is paramount in any relationship. If your sponsor engages you in a sexual relationship, they might not be putting your recovery first. If your sponsor gossips about you, you might be unable to trust that your discussions remain as private as they're meant to be. If your sponsor relapses, you might not feel that their guidance is as sound as it once was. It's your choice on when to part ways; if any of these things happen and you do, no one will object.

A verbally abusive sponsor is another example of one that isn't the best idea. A strict sponsor can be indispensable to your work. A sponsor who calls you names (or berates you) crosses the line from strict to abusive. They should be left behind immediately. A few suggestions here and there aren't bad, but if they insist on giving unsolicited advice, it's time to set boundaries. If your sponsor doesn't respect those boundaries, it's time to find a different one.

The last reason to part with your sponsor is an amicable one. If you feel that your current sponsor has done all they can for your growth and recovery, it's okay to look for someone to guide you into the next phase of your journey. Everyone has a plateau in their knowledge and experience.

Don't dwell on it if you end up parting with your sponsor. Tell them that you'd like to work with someone else. Their lives won't stop because you're moving in another direction.

Keep your focus on your recovery, and don't be guilty that a change of pace is what it took to keep you on the right track. They'll get it because you're both doing the same work. Don't try to go through unnecessary spans of time without a sponsor. If you or your sponsor go out of town, find a substitute you can meet with or call on day one.

We all need help from time to time, and even if your program doesn't technically subscribe to traditional sponsorship, it's still a good idea to have that list of people you can call, meet, and talk to through your journey.

LITERATURE AND STEP WORK

When I say literature, someone's going to have a flashback of that class they didn't mean to take but took and ended up slogging through one of the classics. Or maybe your mind went straight to contemporary literature that was made into a critically acclaimed blockbuster. The literature we'll discuss isn't that kind.

These will be your guides through the program and include hundreds of pages of personal narratives as told by others like us. This literature reads like a manual to step work and shares at a meeting. It's learning material that's applicable through your journey and might raise a question or topic to discuss with your sponsor.

Literature

Let's begin with how reading can help you through recovery. You might say that sounds too simple. Well, there's a reason people have harangued us to read since we started learning to identify letters. Reading of any kind improves your mental health.

By reading this book, you're improving how your brain functions. Whenever we pick up a good fiction or nonfiction read, it engages and stimulates our brains.

Reading also helps give perspective on other points of view, which can then broaden your own. While struggling with addiction, our purview can get a little tunnel-like. Reading helps us expand our line of sight to how someone else thinks or feels and might lead to a change of heart on a topic.

Reading can also expand our minds in other ways. There's a plethora of self-help and philosophical books available. They vary in length, and they might not all be as helpful as we'd like, but there's some insight to be gained there.

Reading on a schedule, say 30 minutes in the morning and an hour before bed, helps maintain a regular schedule throughout our daily lives. The newspaper, a magazine, or any of the program literature we're about to discuss will fit right in as long as you pick it up and give it your attention.

NA has audiobooks and material written in American Sign Language, so there are alternatives to standard text. In addition, some portion of the literature produced by both AA and NA falls into the booklet or pamphlet category. These are bite-sized doses that can fit into that 30 minutes of your morning routine while you sip your good morning beverage.

Let's talk about recovery literature. AA has The Big Book, which is a full guide to the 12 step program. There are print and audio versions of this book available for free online. They also have a shorter version—Twelve Steps and Twelve Traditions. Along with these is a list of pamphlets and their periodical. A complete guide and list can be found online by searching AA literature.

NA has a similar but more detailed online catalog of available literature. Among these are booklets such as White Booklet, which is the group booklet that introduces NA, the steps, and their philosophy on addiction recovery. Twelve Concepts for NA Service is a comprehensive guide to NA's ideas on service and its place in recovery. Basic Text is the guide to NA's program. Other titles of note are It Works: How and Why, Guiding Principles, Living Clean, and Just for Today Meditations.

NA produces a periodical magazine as well. To find a full list, search NA literature, and you'll find their online library. Narratives of past members can also be found in the pages of NA-approved literature, which act as testimonies and guides to the program and recovery.

12 Steps

Let's discuss 12 step programs. They're basically the same for every anonymous group you could join, with adjustments to make them applicable to that program. The reason for the similarity is that addiction is addiction, no matter how it manifests or what you're struggling with.

The 12 steps as listed in The Little White Booklet, Narcotics Anonymous (1986), for example, are:

1. We admitted that we were powerless over our addiction, that our lives had become unmanageable.
2. We came to believe that a Power greater than ourselves could restore us to sanity.
3. We made a decision to turn our will and our lives over to the care of God as we understood Him.
4. We made a searching and fearless moral inventory of ourselves.
5. We admitted to God, to ourselves, and to another human being the exact nature of our wrongs.
6. We were entirely ready to have God remove all these defects of character.
7. We humbly asked Him to remove our shortcomings.
8. We made a list of all persons we had harmed and became willing to make amends to them all.
9. We made direct amends to such people wherever possible, except when to do so would injure them or others.

10. We continued to take personal inventory and when we were wrong promptly admitted it.

11. We sought through prayer and meditation to improve our conscious contact with God as we understood Him, praying only for knowledge of His will for us and the power to carry that out.

12. Having had a spiritual awakening as a result of these steps, we tried to carry this message to addicts, and to practice these principles in all our affairs.

Notice there's a type of action written into each step. This psychological structure makes sense for a disease that has to do with the brain. Recovery is about learning how you got to the point you did and then engaging in new ways to solve problems and cope.

Step work will be a little different for everyone, and there's no time limit or timeframe to work through the 12 steps. The program takes as long as it takes, so have patience with yourself as you learn the ins and outs. What it will mean is getting raw and honest with yourself.

Learning new ways to handle situations and life without your substance tool takes time. Your group, your sponsors, and others in or familiar with the program will have thoughts and suggestions on how to dedicate yourself to the steps and your recovery. There are resources like work-sheets, online forums, and literature, as well.

One thing most people immediately notice about the 12 step program is the seemingly religious slant to the steps. This is actually a spiritual slant as opposed to religious. Different faith models are available for different cultural types. For example, the Native American 12 step program sets the 12 step model into a medicine wheel. NA states in its literature that it is a spiritual, non-religious program.

When AA's founders went about creating their 12 step model, they acknowledged that not everyone would see God the same way or even call their higher power by the same name. As years have progressed, the higher power idea has evolved into what the individual believed it could be. The group, the universe, or nature personified are examples of the spiritual side of 12 step programs.

There are variations on this idea as well. Faith-based recovery groups will utilize the God of their understanding, pertinent to their faith. For those that feel the spiritual side of the 12 step program is a stumbling block, there are more secular styles of the program in practice. These can range from a varied understanding of the higher power model to a scientific stance.

A more scientific slant can be found in the SMART and Moderation Management programs. These programs don't subscribe to the idea of surrender. Instead, they take an empowerment stance and promote the idea that members can take control of their addiction.

While the 12 step program is the most well-known, there are 12 step alternatives offered by the organizations. What has proven the most influential is the idea that like-minded people supporting each other and working toward a common goal get results. The most important part of any program is that you utilize it in a way that is customized to you.

HOME GROUP

A home group is your grounding group where others can get to know you, and absences can be noticed. It gives additional support during extreme life events to help against relapse. In short, this is the meeting you regularly attend, where you learn everyone's names and shares, and it's your place to belong. A home group and a program are the topmost suggestions given for those in recovery.

A home group keeps you accountable. If you're expected to be somewhere or say you'll do something, the knowledge that people you like or trust expect you to stick it out can help you follow through. The ability to stick it out is a vital tool in recovery. You can invest in your home group, and that investment of time and shared experiences give a sense of ownership which will help you to stay committed to the group, possibly for years to come. It's also a unifying feeling to know they're invested in you.

You can make friends. Treatment and the first steps of early recovery can lead to the destruction of your social network. A home group comprises people who've gone through the same thing and have similar goals. Friendships which spring from your feeling of unity can be priceless. Catching a burger or a coffee before or after meeting together demonstrates the awesomeness of fellowship.

One of the things we have to learn how to do in recovery is to have fun sober. Friendship with others in a similar circumstance opens up various ways to relearn how to have fun. For example, you can attend sober birthday parties, sober dances or potlucks, activities, or talk on the phone. Showing up is important to continued recovery and investing in the people who make up your home group motivates you to keep going and trickles out into other parts of your life so that you also show up there.

SERVICE

When you're new to the 12 step program, you're a taker, and that's okay.

You wouldn't be in that seat or in that setting if you didn't conclude that you needed the help. While you learn the ropes and how to navigate your new normal, your primary focus will be figuring everything out. Once you're a little more settled in (still early in your recovery, in case you wondered), I urge you to take notice of what happens in your meeting room.

The simple answer is that you all meet and share in your usual format, but this is one of those times when we need to try for a little more than simple and use our renewed ability to observe. One of the members of your group oversees that meeting. That's your chairperson, and it's a voluntary role. They're not getting paid to guide the meeting or hand out sobriety milestone fobs or chips.

The member that always ends up with the donations hat or basket may be your treasurer. Yet another member might ask for a vote on specific matters or read a report. This is likely your General Service Representative (GSR). They've traveled to represent your group at district committees or area assemblies and returned for your input so that your group is properly represented.

If you show up a little early, you'll find Jim at the empty coffee pot. There's usually coffee at your normal arrival time, and now you've learned that Jim's responsible for it. Get there earlier, and you'll find the same person or people setting out chairs, snacks, and literature to prepare for the upcoming meeting.

All those people, from your chairperson to Jim at the coffee pot, started out where you are as a taker. Then, at some point in their lives, they reached out for help like you did. And there was someone on the other side of that reach who took their hand and helped them up.

That is what service is and how support works. It's yet another tool, and this one comes with an exceptional amount of reward. For quite a while, your world condensed to you, your substance, and what you needed to feel. Now, you're on your way to shifting your focus back out and remembering to take others' feelings and situations into account. That's part of responsibility, and it's also a part of service.

There are service opportunities within your home group. The longer you're with your group, the more you might feel the need to do something more. Positions like chair or secretary, treasurer, or GSR are rotating voluntary positions. The length of time each person holds a position varies from group to group and will depend on how often your group meets. You could join the setup group, prepare the room, or even help Jim with the coffee. If you don't have a Jim and coffee's the last thing done, take on that responsibility. If there isn't coffee, you can help set up the chairs. Be the Jim for your group, and you'll be pleasantly surprised by the way you feel as a result.

You may have the opportunity to do a panel. Panel members speak at schools, prisons, hospitals, detox centers, or treatment centers and share their experiences, strengths, and hopes. A panel leader may ask for volunteers.

This is the point where you might say you're too busy, but you'd be surprised by the time you have to spend if you look for it. If you have the opposite problem and find too much time on your hands, a service commitment will help fill your time. Whether it's those few minutes before a meeting to make coffee or getting notes at a meeting, you can be sure it's something you will find rewarding. As a bonus, a service commitment will have a similar result as having a home group. You'll feel motivated to show up on time and do what you've said you would.

The gift of service keeps giving back to you in other ways. The more you donate your time and skills, the more you put yourself into the world. You might find new hobbies and interests. You could also expand your new network of friends. You'll notice that the more often you spend your time in service, the further away you grow from the troubled person and place you used to be.

You could ultimately be the one that reaches out and offers someone a hand up. The principle of the 12th step in every program is that in order to work it, you must try to help others. Sharing your hope, experiences, and strength ensures that the program will be there for the next group of people. In this step, you can offer a ride to someone who might not attend the meeting otherwise and follow up with them a few days later. Then, you can do the setup, which sets an example. This is the basis behind the attraction factor of the program as opposed to promotion.

Deep into his recovery, a young man looked for a way to give back and chose to be a recovery coach. This is a position in which some training is involved; they take calls and meet people to help them find the best route to recovery.

He posted on social media about his new service undertaking and received a message from an old friend. The friend was in bad shape and desperate for help. This was a person from the young man's past, who shared his addiction and substance of choice, and when they met, he was very rough. The young man used his training and got his friend into a program. The two fell out of touch. A few months later, they bumped into each other, and the friend had been clean and healthy for nine months.

The young man was relieved, proud, but also humbled. One of the things you learn in a 12 step program is that "you can't keep what you have without giving it away." Through this young man's outreach training, he was able to help his friend and remind himself of how he was before recovery. Keeping the progress, you've gained in recovery sometimes boils down to facing how things were by seeing someone else who's there and being the hand that helps them up to begin their recovery.

Affirmations

- I am strong and brave, and I can do this.
- I listen to others that came before me and reach out for guidance.

4

STOP BLAME, TAKE SUGGESTIONS, BE GRATEFUL

I don't blame anybody but myself. I did it because I wanted to do it. Never blame, because if you blame... you need to go back to rehab... that means you didn't get it.

— NAOMI CAMPBELL

One of the things that we've mentioned is learning new ways to have fun. The blame game is not a new game. It's a broken recording that can prove a mountainous stumbling block if not dealt with.

Blaming someone for something you've done or that has affected your life is a way of passing judgment on that person and making them less important than you. Whatever it is they've done, it's their responsibility to fix.

It's time to derail that train. Then, to move forward in recovery, casting blame on others will have to become a thing of the past. This is part of the responsibility tool, and it's an important one to catch.

The types of blame are varied. The grandiose idea means that the individual placing the blame has an inflated idea of themselves. Those who place this kind of blame have a hard time accepting criticism and quickly shift the focus to blame someone else. Those with excessive grandiosity might have a mental health disorder called narcissistic personality disorder.

Self-blame is when we take whatever happened and turn it all on us. This is particularly prevalent in cases of trauma. In this situation, the person takes full responsibility because it gives them a type of control over whether it might happen again. To derail this type of blame, the person has to accept that they were not responsible, and while we want the world to be just, that's often not the case.

Victim blaming happens when the person most affected by the situation, the victim, is held responsible for all parts of it. When addiction first gained notice, this was a common way to view it and might still linger in some areas. However, once the definition of addiction shifted to that of a chronic illness, much of this type of blame went with it. That doesn't mean that we're not responsible. On the contrary, taking responsibility for our recovery allows us to regain our power in the face of a disease over which we're powerless.

If we can't let blame go, our emotional sobriety is put at risk. Much like forgiveness, the fallout from holding onto the blame game will stunt our work moving forward. We're creating excuses and allowing reasons for relapse. Even if we don't relapse, our personal narrative and continued negative self-talk become that of the dry drunk. This sort of justification can range from "My job's really stressful, and I need to relax," to "All of my friends support my habit," or "This really bad thing happened in my childhood, so I have to cope."

There are parts of that narrative that aren't your fault. If you experienced trauma or a dozen other circumstances dictated by your environment as opposed to choice, there wasn't much control to be exerted over that situation. The part we have to control is ourselves. Casting blame holds us back from everything, including recovery.

To effectively disembark the blame game, we need to admit our mistakes. Not easy or fun, but it's important to be responsible for the things that we control. Counseling can help us give up the blame and push forward with a new outlook. Our mistakes can become learning experiences if we take away the habit of reactionary blame that masks them.

ZIP IT AND LISTEN

It's time to be serious again because this next tool is a serious help to recovery of all kinds and perspectives. We've realized through hitting bottom and seeking treatment that what we were doing before wasn't working. We had gotten into an unmanageable situation, and when we're that lost, all we want is for someone to tell us how to get out of it—to suggest a fix.

As we gain tools and start to regain steadier footing, our need for suggestions can begin to diminish. Yes, the tools we're given help us regain our power, but with power comes responsibility. One of those responsibilities is to acknowledge that we won't see everything or understand it when it comes.

What do I mean, and what's this tool I'm talking about? Let's start with the meaning. As we regain some semblance of steadiness, we gain confidence. This, in itself, is a good thing. What can happen, though, is that when we regain our confidence, we stop listening.

That will not help you five minutes, five months, or five years from now. The tool I'm referring to is a subtle one—it's listening to and taking suggestions. Think about that sentence for a second. Listening to and taking suggestions is how you started this road. The wisdom that's gotten you this far hasn't changed. If anything, it's opened the door to gain more of it and in varied perspectives. To remain diligent in our recovery, we need to retain the ability to take suggestions from those who've gone before us and those struggling with us. If we keep this tool sharp, we're less likely to grow complacent in the future.

Since we're on the topic, there are a couple of suggestions that you should take early on. When we leave treatment, we're given a list of suggestions or recommendations. The idea behind these is to sandbag our early recovery stages against the flood that's going to happen. The most common of these suggestions is to continue attending meetings and connecting with your sponsor.

In fact, if you've gone through treatment, you've heard the suggestion "90 in 90." This refers to 90 meetings in 90 days. Let's recall our conversation about our brains. We've tricked them, explored the paths, and identified some of the compounds naturally created in them. Did you know that it takes around 90 days to develop a habit? This is because it takes about 90 days to establish a new pattern of behavior in our brains.

So, for the newcomer, fresh from relapse, or anyone starting to slip, 90 in 90 is a useful suggestion and tool. It counts as a tool because we're establishing or reestablishing a habit. All you do is get yourself to a meeting each day for 90 days, and the rewards of your new habit will find you.

You'll meet people who will keep you from feeling isolated from the loss of your old network while you wait for your current network to heal enough to become strong support. It's a safe place even while you're vulnerable and in the early stages. You'll find others in those rooms willing to have a bite to eat, exchange numbers, or give you a ride in case you need them.

The 90 in 90 suggestion is something you can accomplish tomorrow or 90 days from now instead of someday. Achieving 90 meetings in 90 days adds a few more habits. Sobriety becomes a habit. Reaching out to friends and family becomes a habit. Communicating and interacting becomes a habit. In 90 days, bad habits are replaced with several healthy habits, so this is a suggestion to take seriously.

GRATITUDE

Since we've visited our river several times, the one that floods when it rains, let's take a moment and go to the beach instead. Envision whatever beach comes to mind. It doesn't have to be the ocean. It could be a lakeside beach or a spit of sand alongside a deep pool of water in the river. As long as it's calm, tranquil, and quiet, maybe rhythmic, that's the scenery we're going for. Hold on to that vision for as long as it takes for you to smell it, almost taste it, and that's when you smile.

We took a moment and remembered a place and probably a time, which made us feel better and smile. This is the idea behind gratitude in the simplest terms. Recall that we discussed taking one day at a time so we could be present for the moments when happiness happens. Gratitude is the tool we use to transform the experience of those happy moments into strength. It means being thankful, actively glad, and grateful to have that moment.

There will be times when we are tested during our recovery. We'll have dark moments or miss goals we've set for ourselves. For example, maybe you didn't make it to your meeting as you planned. Maybe that guy in traffic took too long to notice the light change, and you were late to work. Perhaps you had a big presentation and spilled half your coffee on your clothes 30 seconds before go time. Maybe you (insert your stressor here), and life seems like crap, so now you can't get your substance out of your head.

It happens because life is messy sometimes, people make mistakes, and we all have those days when that last straw has us teetering. This is when the strength you've built up on the good days is important. This is when the training you've put your brain through needs to take over and offer a different focus. This is also when you might need to make that phone call to your sponsor, trusted friend, or loved one for a reminder that there's something to be grateful for.

Did I say we've trained our brains to seek out gratitude? Yes, and the way that we cultivate this tool might be given to us in treatment, through our sponsor, or in a piece of literature. Practicing gratitude is an activity that engages the prefrontal cortex of our brains. The prefrontal cortex is the part of our brain that controls learning and decision-making processes. When we practice gratitude, we refocus on positive feelings, and when we "give it away" with gratitude, it inspires a lasting change in the activity of our prefrontal cortex.

Gratitude can also positively affect our physical, mental, and emotional health. Studies show a marked reduction in relapse for those who practice gratitude (The Power of Gratitude in Your Recovery, 2021). We keep a better emotional outlook. We stay more involved in our programs and program promises, leading to greater social support. We also have less stress and negative health reactions.

In fact, practicing gratitude can help strengthen relationships and increase resilience and trauma recovery. It can increase our likelihood to exercise and do other healthy things, boost our immune system, help us sleep, and lower our blood pressure. It could also reduce the likelihood of depression and anxiety. We could also see an increase in our optimism, pleasure, and joy, which means we're generally happier and more satisfied.

Practicing gratitude does take work. There are people in the world that have or hold a naturally positive outlook on life. This can waver, and for those of us who've had a lot of negatives in our lives, it can be a foreign idea to seek the positive. It might be a new idea to you, but the benefits sound pretty good.

To start, you want to make gratitude a focal point. There are a few tricks you can use to talk your brain into this. One of these is a gratitude journal. They take a few different forms, such as a list of three good things about the day. The bare minimum for this is two. Handwriting this list will help reinforce it, so pick up a new notebook, decorate the front however you'd like if you're so inclined, and start on page one.

If you look at those blank lines and have nothing to write, prompts are available online for such an occurrence. Otherwise, you can start with general things like breathing or seeing. The idea is to choose what you feel grateful for, and even if that's tough, to begin with, as you practice gratitude, you'll start to feel it as well.

Another way to practice gratitude is through mindfulness. In this iteration, mindfulness is being in the moment. For example, if you're doing dishes, be aware of the temperature and smoothness of the water, the prickle of the soap, and the sweet smell when the bubbles burst. Keep your mind on your task and from wandering to the things you need to do or problems. Focusing on the task you're in allows your mind to settle down and engage the logical side while calming your emotional reactions.

Embracing your imperfections is another tactic in gratitude practice. Mistakes will happen, plans will go askew, or you might miss your meeting. Instead of dwelling on what you've done wrong, think of the things that went right. Maybe you aced a midterm, or your presentation went exactly as planned despite the coffee on your shirt. Celebrate these things with gratitude. If things are rougher, think back to a time when you achieved something, reflect on it, and allow yourself to be grateful that it happened. Imagine the events that led to your achievement and what would've happened if that event had gone differently.

Embrace the positive in the situation. When delays happen, refocus your attention from what's gone wrong to what's right about it. For example, if you're out to eat and service is poor or slow, recognize that you're able to be there and enjoy the energy, the warmth or coolness, the company you're with, and the fact that when your food arrives, you'll be full.

Gratitude is synonymous with thankfulness, and one of the ways to practice gratitude is to show your thanks. Whether this is by thanking someone for their help, their ear, or their presence or by going a step further and writing thank you cards, thanking others will help you feel thankful. If you choose thank you cards, they don't have to be elaborate. A note of thanks and why is more than enough.

Volunteering is another way to practice gratitude. In the same way that we "give it away to keep it," when we engage in volunteer programs that we're passionate about, we're reminded of what we have. Paying it forward to others is a bonus, and we can be grateful that we're able to do it.

So, by practicing gratitude and training our minds toward a more positive process, we're taking our positive self-talk to the next level. It's moved beyond us into positive focus and positive action. When we actively engage our brain, our brain learns and grows until it shifts from its negative patterns into more positive lanes. When we have those dark, crazy days, we can pull out our gratitude journal for a reminder or practice mindfulness, and our logical mind will follow its new path to positive solutions. If your sobriety still feels uncertain after doing those two things, make that phone call and talk it out. Later, you can practice gratitude for the person that took your call.

FORGIVENESS AND SELF-LOVE

Let's say that your child takes the last cookie without asking and that you planned to have that cookie after finishing a particularly tedious or strenuous task. Are you going to hold it against your child for eating your cookie? Maybe for a second, but if your child didn't know that was your plan, you'll forgive them and buy or make more cookies for you both to enjoy. You let it go and move on.

Learning forgiveness and self-love can be a little harder. Forgiveness is another term that's often associated with religion. It's a common theme in most Christian literature; however, forgiveness is not about religion or related dogma. It's about letting the past go, accepting what happened, and moving forward from it rather than having it drag like chains around you. Forgiveness is rarely about whether the other person deserves it. We're human, and we're all going to make mistakes. The point of forgiveness is to allow all of the anger, fear, guilt, and grief caused by a mistake to dissipate and make room for better feelings and a better future.

Forgiving ourselves can be the toughest of all the situations and people in our lives that we might need to forgive at one time or another. Yet, forgiveness is another powerful tool in your new toolkit. To fully commit to your new road to recovery, you'll have to forgive the lengths you went to and the things that happened while in full addiction mode. Remember, addiction is like any other disease when left untreated; its fallout can get pretty deep and distracting.

How can you go about forgiving yourself? Well, there are a few steps that might make this a little simpler. First, we'll need to gain some clarity on what we face. We need to explore the actual triggers that led us into addiction and how we feel about it. Some parts of that will probably make us angry in the present, which is why counseling to find clarity is highly recommended. Counseling can help us figure out how to express and put those emotions in a healthy atmosphere.

Next, we have to accept what we've done in the past and also accept that it's in the past. It happened, we were that person with those beliefs and morals, but that isn't who we are anymore. You can let it go, forgive yourself, and move more firmly forward into who and how you are now.

We should learn to be compassionate and grateful to ourselves. Showing ourselves gratitude for undertaking recovery helps us to see ourselves in a more positive light and counts as positive self-talk. Be glad that you were strong and undertook recovery no matter how slowly it may progress or how difficult it is at times. That's where having compassion for yourself comes in. Understand that the process isn't easy, and we'll make mistakes. However, if you show yourself compassion, you can learn to handle stress in healthier ways. Expressing our struggles and the emotions connected to them keeps us from falling into old habits and back into negative self-talk.

We have to look at what we regret the most. This isn't a personal boxing match where we exchange swings with decisions and situations that make us cringe. Instead, this is an evaluation of who we were and why that decision now bothers us. Once we've discerned our greatest regrets, we can define our current beliefs and morals. Knowing how differently we approach things now instead of how we used to can help us let go of the guilt tied to those regrets. We've evaluated them, learned from them, and now we can move on from them.

Once accomplished, all that work spent forgiving ourselves opens the door for self-love. This is another key tool to place in your toolkit and can also be a little difficult. If you're good with yourself, look at the people around you. It's much easier to love yourself with support, and when we love ourselves, it's easier to love others. We can't give away what we don't have.

To continue to develop self-love, we undertake and build a self-care routine. We can take the energy we used to maintain our addiction and channel it into caring for ourselves. Things like exercise, finding hobbies that mean something to us, visiting with positive role models, eating healthier, meditation or prayer, rest or relaxation, and maintaining good hygiene are all things that benefit us and consume some of our extra energy. In addition, exercise, rest or relaxation, and maintaining good hygiene also improve the way that we see ourselves.

Secondly, you have to learn how to forgive others and let go of resentment. This can be as tough as forgiving ourselves, particularly if traumatic experiences are tied to a person. So, to clarify, and this goes for both types of forgiveness, this isn't handing out excuses, leveling blame, or condoning past actions. Instead, this kind of forgiveness is letting go of negative emotions and situations to create space for positivity, clarity, and sobriety.

Playing the blame game and holding onto resentment for things others have or haven't done is a common way for us to rationalize. The trouble is holding grudges against people for not meeting our expectations, trauma, telling us what to do, perceived hypocrisy and lies, letting us down, manipulations, authority figures, and those who don't love us back don't help us. It certainly doesn't foster good networks.

Harboring resentments can have a debilitating effect on our recovery. If we don't let these things go, we might use them later to rationalize relapse. We might use them as an excuse to not take full responsibility. We might continue to allow negative feelings and self-talk. It could end up hurting our new relationships.

There are a few ways to work through our resentment toward others and ultimately forgive them.

- Identify your underlying emotions. Whether this is anger or something else, if we don't know how we feel about something, we can't completely let it go.
- Actively engage with your anger or resentment. Denial isn't going to help anyone, not even that river in Egypt. If you don't acknowledge how you feel toward a person or circumstance, it will only fester into an excuse or stumbling block.
- Identify how what you said or did, impacted the situation. Very few times in life exist when only one side or person is responsible for a situation. If the situation bothers you, explore what your part was and how that might have led to the outcome.
- Practice healthy expression. Put your anger into words in a journal, play sports to relieve stress, or pump all that extra energy into exercise. It's not doing any good by seething in the back of your mind.

- Show compassion for yourself and others. Remember, we're all human, and we all make mistakes.
- Resentment is not a team sport. If you find yourself in a situation where things turn negative, see yourself out. This invites you to allow negativity back into your life. When we're trying to establish positive self-talk and forgiveness, rehashing old wounds in a circular fashion only worsens them. If you talk it out, that's good, but don't keep returning to that rut. It's not forgiveness if you keep repeating the problem but don't let it go.
- Make peace with your past. Acknowledge it happened, identify your feelings about it, and let it go.
- Devote time to understanding and developing what you need emotionally.
- Try to put yourself in their situation.
- Take responsibility for your feelings. They're yours, and no matter how sour, you might as well own them.
- Allow yourself to forgive others and yourself.
- Use I in place of you to stop accusations before they start. "I feel that…" or "I believe that…."
- Give yourself room to express the good stuff that might've been on lockdown through your addiction. Things like hugging and healing are good things.

- Being of service and helping others will also help to ease your anger toward others. This offers perspective.
- Have an open mind. Keeping an open mind allows for change.

Another type of forgiveness we all have in common is the forgiveness of others for us. Family and friends affected by things we did while chasing our substance of choice need room to heal just like we do. The more they learn about the disease of addiction, the better able they'll be to understand what happened. We have to give them the same patience and time that we give ourselves so that they can move forward into a new chapter and view. If they set new, healthy boundaries, we should respect them.

Affirmations

- I am grateful for my recovery.
- I give myself permission to feel my feelings.

5

RELAPSE PREVENTION

Staying sober really was the most important thing in my life now and had given me direction when I thought I had none.

— ERIC CLAPTON

Before we get too far into relapse prevention, let's take a minute to acknowledge that relapse happens. This is not a failure, even if our first instinct is to frame it as one. Relapse percentages are about the same for addiction as those of any chronic illness. The important thing to do is figure out how to acknowledge and take responsibility for our mistake and learn from it.

One way to increase our effectiveness in maintaining our recovery is to acquaint ourselves with the warning signs of relapse and to use our experiences to learn what triggers us. When we have a grasp on what relapse might look like, we can utilize our tools to combat it to retain sobriety and recovery.

When most of us think about relapse, we jump straight to substance use. If relapse or a near miss is part of your journey, one or more of these warning signs is going to look familiar. There are other warning signs that, once you read them, you'll have a light bulb moment. If this is your first round, pay close attention to the emotional, physical, and mental changes that signal a possible relapse.

If your emotional state grows compromised, it can affect your likelihood of relapse even without you realizing it. Your reason for entering recovery and all the drama that addiction brought into your world might still be strong enough memories that you're not considering a return trip. If you find yourself bottling up your feelings, isolating yourself, skipping therapy or meetings, being unwilling to share at meetings, or keeping poor nutrition and sleep habits, pay attention. These are all signs that your emotional state isn't in fighting form. A long talk with a counselor or other trusted person might be needed to decipher the underlying problem.

The mental stages are accompanied by discontent in your recovery progress, restlessness with a devolving routine, and weighing the pros and cons of returning to substance. Those trains of thought lead to cravings for your substance of choice, excessive thoughts of people, places, and things related to the substance, minimizing or glamorizing how it used to be, bargaining and lying, creating ways to control future use, being on the lookout for opportunities to relapse, and fantasizing or planning for relapse. Noticing any or some of these signs means you need to take action and utilize your support network to devise ways to subvert your slip and protect your recovery.

The physical stage is the simplest. It's a return to substance use. This can be once or over an extended period of time. Full relapse carries danger with it. You've been clean for a while, and if you use the same amount of substance you did before you began recovery, it can lead to an overdose. One last time has killed more than a few people in recovery because their resistance to the substance has dropped from their time spent sober.

PLAY THE TAPE

We've tricked our brains in a few different ways thus far, but what happens when your brain tricks you back? It happens, and it's particularly common in early recovery. This is one of those situations when our brain uses selective memory, the way that Joe uses selective hearing to get out of his honey-do list to go on his fishing trip. Our brains are even more insidious than good old Joe.

Say you're doing something you've done hundreds of times. It can be a simple, mundane thing like barbecuing, cutting the grass, or folding the laundry. You work up a sweat, or your energy for the task starts to ebb away. You want refreshment, a little energy boost, or whatever fits to get it done. Enter your brain.

You're abruptly assaulted with an image of an ice-cold beer or a supercharged rush from another substance. Maybe all that's on your mind is winding down, and that calm, euphoric feeling overtakes the video feed in your head. There is the substance, there is the feeling, and the video of your initial response is stuck on repeat. This is called euphoric recall, which means remembering only the good things about something while selectively ignoring the negative. That sounds like trouble, but there are tools for this.

When euphoric recall replays in your head, it's time to confront your selective memory with the truth you know that follows. We've been down that road, and yeah, that first frame looks amazing, but it's only the first frame of the tape. You need to play that tape through to the end. Play it to what happens next. We know this story, so you need to forget the pretty loop and keep going.

What happens next is that our disease initializes. One becomes five, and then it's a crap shoot from that point on. Then comes the blackouts, arguments, brawls, tears, guilt, shame, legal repercussions, broken bones, hospitalizations, jail cells, and death.

Push the play button on that tape until there's no more to play. Play it all the way to the inevitable end and when you've finished, grab a coffee, take a nap or a walk, or meditate to relax. When you get to the end of your sober alternative, you'll look forward to your next 12 step meeting and seeing your sober friends. Those alternatives are much better than the trauma and drama that addiction brings, which we've all been through. When we learn to play the tape through to the end, we expose that euphoric frame for the selective memory trick it is. Playing the tape and utilizing the tools we've learned at meetings and through treatment gives us the edge we need to hold on to our lives.

TRIGGER AWARENESS

The word trigger has come up a few times already. A trigger in addiction is any environment, social, or emotional situation that makes us think of substance use in our past. Triggers don't necessarily lead straight to relapse, but they can cause cravings by sparking those memories.

Triggers differ from person to person and aren't always easy to spot. They can be broken down into external and internal types. Of the two, external triggers are easier to pinpoint. They're physical-people, places, and things-that remind us of our days before recovery. Internal triggers are more complex since they're tied to simple things like routines or feelings, good and bad, that we use substance to cope with or celebrate.

Awareness of your triggers is as important as knowing the difference between a trigger and a high-risk situation. A high-risk situation is when we're exposed to our substance or substance use. We've discussed that abstinence is key and the potential of shifting addiction from one substance to another. A high-risk situation caters to one or both of these possibilities, meaning that your substance or a potential substitute is readily available.

We'll start with the top 10 triggers, the first of which is HALT. Hungry, Angry, Lonely, or Tired (HALT) management is as simple as making sure you eat regularly, practice mindfulness, seek social support, and have a regular sleep schedule. If your basic needs are met, you're better able to cope with situations of any kind.

We all face challenging emotions during our lives. Anger, grief, and sadness might have been the reason we used substance as a coping tool. Learning new ways to cope with these emotions is key to keeping our recovery on track. Therapy can offer tools and support to help with this. Stress, be it chronic or acute, is another one that requires new coping skills to manage.

Renewed self-confidence is a good thing, but overconfidence can lead to trouble. It's important to retain some humility during our recovery, no matter how long it's lasted, because there will be triggers that could catch you off guard. This is when the "just one" slips into our self-talk because we're in control, but the trouble is that one is never enough. If we forget that, we might find ourselves slipping quickly.

Illness, either physical or mental, can stress the body. Dealing with pain, depression, or anxiety can increase the number of triggers that affect us. When you go to the doctor for any health concern, be sure to mention that you are a recovering addict. This way, you and your doctor can discuss treatment options that won't include addictive prescriptions or high-risk medications.

Social isolation comes from the anxiety and exhaustion that we might feel engaging in social activities without the help of our former tool. Starting with a sponsor or trusted friend is a good way to get started and mitigate the danger of complete isolation. The idea is to start small and expand. You'll have a group of like-minded people to expand to, even if it's one at a time.

Romantic relationships can be messy and, when they end, devastating. It's highly recommended that people new to recovery not engage in romantic relationships for their first year.

Good things, like a promotion or a new job, can be as triggering as bad things. This is the celebratory trigger; coping with it is simplest by planning sober parties. Good things can also unlock a new level of stress and anxiety over performance or responsibilities, so you'll need to engage your new stress coping strategies to offset those triggers.

Nostalgia is a thing. There have been songs about it, and it can be easy to remember the good points and forget the trouble that came along with our substance use. If your mind gets stuck on repeat, reach out to your network, counselor, or sponsor, so they can remind you why you chose recovery to begin with.

The places and situations that might trigger you belong on your list, especially if they might devolve into high-risk scenarios. In this situation, forewarned is forearmed, and you can make logical choices or use your exit strategy to upend their impact.

Other triggers include people, places, and objects. Other people, like former dealers, coworkers, employers, neighbors, or a partner or spouse, might say or suggest things that cause a craving. Places like certain neighborhoods, clubs or bars, worksites, hotels, highway exits, or downtown areas might remind you of when or where you found your substance. Objects like furniture, cash or cards, empty pill bottles, TV and movie ads, and paraphernalia could all spark a memory and cravings.

You'll notice that some of these triggers can fall into more than one environmental, social, or emotional category. They can also fall into both internal and external trigger types. The thing to be aware of is that, like our recovery, our triggers are individual. With that in mind, there are a few strategies and tools that we can utilize to minimize the effect that triggers and high-risk situations have on our recovery.

It all starts with awareness and having a plan. This is another highly recommended suggestion and one of those times when it's best to be prepared for a rainy day. You'll need to sit down, preferably with your sponsor, and list possible high-risk scenarios and triggers. You want an outside view because they might come up with a few things you can't or make a suggestion that reminds you of a situation you wouldn't have remembered otherwise. Daily life is full of things that might spark a craving or memory, so having a way to deal with that situation will safeguard your recovery.

The best idea for handling high-risk situations is not to put yourself in them, but as that's not always an option, the next best idea is to have an exit strategy. For example, a company dinner or a wedding with an open bar might turn into a high-risk situation in no time. It's best to have someone to call, a way to step out or away from the situation or to bring support with you.

To avoid triggers, you'll need to take it personally and then expand. Delete any numbers on your phone that you no longer need and stick to socializing with people who have what you want - recovery. You'll need to redefine your idea of fun to fit your recovery. If you slip, let go of the guilt and learn from your mistake. Examine what happened and why you were triggered so that you can craft a coping strategy for the next time. That's what learning is all about. Lastly, we have to get used to discomfort. The world and society won't change because we've undertaken recovery. There will be situations and comments that cause us to crave, and all we can do is manage it until our craving passes.

So, what if we're triggered or taken off guard? Well, you need to maintain your support system so that when something happens, you have someone to reach out to. You don't even have to talk about the problem; just talk until the craving passes.

Another way to handle this is through distraction. These days, distractions are easy to come by. If you can't take a walk, play a game on your phone or watch a video.

We've discussed the idea of self-talk off and on throughout the book, and this is another coping strategy to deal with sudden triggers. Give yourself a pep talk in the form of a logical reminder that you recognize this is a trigger, that you're doing what you can to avoid it, and that it does not control you.

Whenever possible, practice relaxation. Step away (I go to a bathroom; you can find one almost anywhere) and take a few breaths to regroup. This doesn't have to be full meditation. The idea is to alleviate your stress before it becomes overwhelming. The stressors in our lives can be quick, but if we practice relaxation, we can remain relaxed in any situation.

PUT RECOVERY FIRST

Let's talk about plans, priorities, and time. There will be a few numbers in this section, but they're simple ones. The first is seven - there are seven days in a week. The second is 24 - there are 24 hours in each day of that week. We're already approaching both of those numbers one day at a time. Why bring it up again?

Those two numbers have a constant and lasting effect on your recovery. We're going to take an unpretty walk down memory lane for this. Remember back when our addiction was in full control? Now, think about how many of those 24 hours you spent on acquiring and using. How many of those seven days were devoted to it? Think about the lengths you'd have gone to get your substance.

Our answers to those questions are now the amount of time we have to give to our recovery. The time we spent finding, using, and maintaining is now free of substance demands. It makes sense that we'd devote the same amount of time to recovery. We'd do anything back then to satisfy a craving, so now we need to do anything to keep our recovery. Recovery is our priority, and as such, it requires both a plan and time devoted to it.

The Plan

We're going to start with a safety plan which is also called a crisis plan. A safety plan is how you utilize your coping mechanisms, exit strategies, and awareness of triggers to prevent relapse. It's going to change as you change, so be sure that, as you progress through your recovery, you revisit your safety plan and update it to match where you are. Your safety plan isn't going to look like Joe's or Meg's because it's yours, just like your recovery won't look like theirs. Sure, we'll have similarities, but no two people are the same, so no two triggers and no two safety plans will be the same.

A common theme in substance use is to self-medicate. This can be from underlying mental health issues or as a coping tool during tough situations. When crises arise in our lives, no matter how long we've been in recovery, our tricky brains will likely jump straight to substance to cope with or medicate the problem. It's like your favorite sweater or comfortable shoes, a well-worn and familiar solution to problems. In this case, we know that substance isn't going to help, which is why we have a plan in place. Since our tricky brains might nudge us hard enough to slip, our plan will also have the next steps to take after a slip or relapse so we can be prepared to return to recovery.

We already have the tools to craft and utilize our safety plan. We're now familiar with the warning signs of relapse, and we have an idea of coping mechanisms to deal with our list of acknowledged triggers. We know our high-risk situations.

The next piece of our puzzle is cravings. Like our triggers and high-risk situations, we need to be aware of what our cravings feel like, whether physical or emotional. By identifying these cravings and how they affect us, we can utilize our tools to manage them. So, with triggers, high-risk situations, and cravings all listed, the next step is to identify all the tools in our toolbox. While we make this list, we should pay special attention to how using one or more tools has helped us cope in the past. This will play an important role in forming our safety plan and can be as simple as calling a friend, regular support meeting attendance, exercising, becoming immersed in nature, or having regular check-ins with a peer, mentor, or therapist.

The final piece of our puzzle is having and using an exit strategy if a holiday soiree becomes a different kind of party or any number of other scenarios where leaving is the best choice. Examples of exit strategy would be having a friend on standby to pick you up. Their arrival is your opportunity to exit. Alternatively, take a friend with you, and the two of you can leave together.

When all is said and done, your safety plan should include the warning signs, all your triggers and cravings, all of your tools to deal with each, and exit strategies. Your plan is impressive on paper, but it's only effective if you use it. There will come times when you need it, which is why we update it to match our progress and the changes in our lives as they affect cravings, triggers, and tools.

The Priorities

When we took that unpretty trip down memory lane, one of the things that we might have noticed was how great a priority our substance was. In recovery, self-care gains status on our priority list. For many of us, that means we have to relearn how to take care of ourselves. Self-care is the maintenance of the physical, mental, emotional, and spiritual levels. That's four levels of care, and it might seem a little overwhelming to begin with but think of it as loops of the same being that tie together and help each other.

Self-care is taking care of your needs, which means your health and wellness. Physically speaking, this is practicing good hygiene, which can slip away when addiction is in full swing. Brushing our teeth and hair, bathing regularly, and keeping our environment healthy are all simple ways to take care of our bodies.

It's also important to be mindful of what our body needs and to satisfy those needs in healthy ways. Adding nutritious meals and drinks will give us more energy and will also have a positive effect on our mental health. Exercise and activity help us get back into shape and relieve stress, anxiety, or pent-up frustration. Mindfulness also means awareness of how well you sleep. A quiet environment and the right type of bed will affect your quality of sleep.

When we delay or ignore what our body asks for, we practice poor self-care. If we're injured, we should see a doctor sooner than later. If we're hungry, have a snack. If we're restless, we need to find something productive to do. This is also the time to address any lingering medical concerns which might have been masked or caused by our substance use. Keeping ourselves healthy, scheduling enjoyable exercises or activities, and eating and drinking with nutrition in mind will boost our immunity and self-confidence.

Be as mindful of your mental health as your physical. The warning signs of depression or anxiety might require a trip to therapy to learn coping strategies that work for you. If something doesn't work, bring it up so that other options can be explored. Self-care also means advocating for yourself so that you can utilize the right strategies for yourself. In the instance of a dual diagnosis, awareness of a secondary condition can be enough to understand and utilize new coping methods.

Connecting, listening, and learning with or from others is another way to practice mental self-care. Engaging with other people in groups, with friends, coworkers, or with family can open up new understanding about addiction, treatment, and recovery. While you're connecting, be sure to set healthy boundaries. Setting healthy boundaries keeps us from getting overwhelmed and helps us to manage obligations and prioritize our time. This is when we can remind others to communicate with respect, take everyone's feelings into account, and give space if needed. Setting and maintaining limits can help reduce negative situations, which can impact recovery.

Learning new skills in a group or individually is another way to practice mental self-care. These can be learned at work, through a hobby, or in a therapy class. Any activity that expands our minds also adds to our self-confidence and satisfaction.

Spiritual self-care requires daily maintenance. When we learn to address our spiritual self, we gain strength which can be utilized during setbacks in our recovery. This can be in the form of individual or group wellness activities. Meditation or spending time connecting with nature are ways to take care of our spirit. Group prayer or service can also help and can keep us from isolating. Another type of spiritual care that can be done in a group is yoga, which combines body, mind, and spirit into its perspective and has multiple skill levels as well.

The Time

We're going to utilize the time we spent seeking and using our substance to prioritize our recovery. We have a safety plan so we can cope when uncertain situations arise. We're practicing self-care, so we've devoted a little of our time to our physical, mental, emotional, and spiritual well-being. There's still time to fill in our days. Seconds, minutes, and hours which work, family obligations, and our new routines don't quite manage.

This, along with our self-care, is the time that we put recovery first. These are the times to do "the next right thing" even when it doesn't feel like the right thing to do. Self-discovery is one of the continuous highlights of recovery. It takes work to keep growing and learning, and that is work we need to put into ourselves.

We're going to dedicate our time to self-improvement instead of indulgence. Unfortunately, there's not an easy way to define one from the other. If things continue to improve, you're on the right track. If things start to go south, we've slipped into indulgence, and it's time to reset and try again. When we seek self-improvement, we stop competing against others and compete against who we used to be instead.

Recovery first is the most important form of self-care. We're no longer trying to conform to the world. It's okay to work on ourselves and let the world adapt to us. The fact is, we can't love or take care of others if we can't love and care for ourselves first. When we place our focus on recovery, we make it possible to take care of others simply through being of service. As long as we continue to devote time and prioritize our recovery first, our self-awareness and self-improvement will continue as well.

Beware of complacency. Time and again, we've said that recovery is work. There might be a time when we feel that the work is done or that other things need more attention. This kind of shift in our priorities can lead to a slippery slope of complacency. When we stop working the steps and stop working on ourselves, we run the risk of relapse or becoming a dry drunk. Even if you've been through all 12 steps, it's beneficial to revisit them so that we don't forget where we started and end up back there again.

Affirmations

- I am able to do anything when I am clean and sober.
- I am changing for the better each and every day.

6

SPIRITUAL PRINCIPLES AND AWAKENINGS

It gives you a beautiful serenity. It's a cornerstone of recovery because it changes consciousness.

— RUSSELL BRAND

U nless you belong to a SMART 12 step program that utilizes different tools, most programs will reference God or a higher power. In fact, recognition of a higher power, as you understand it, is usually the second tradition built into any program.

Aside from reasons such as having something greater than yourself, you might wonder what the spiritual side of the program has to do with anything. Well, let's reconsider our brain and the dopamine excreted by it. In a normal brain, this happens naturally anytime we do anything fun. In other brains, this feel-good chemical is an elusive fairytale. A brain affected by substance has an even more difficult time creating its own dopamine.

Most of the highs that we seek flood our neural receptors with dopamine which means that, eventually, we need more substance to experience the same pleasure. It also means that pleasurable things unrelated to substance sometimes no longer create a blip on the pleasure scale and that the paths built by our dopamine-seeking highs deepen into trenches. How does the spiritual factor into brain chemistry?

We'll begin with prayer and meditation. Accepting and seeking a power higher than ourselves gives us an understanding that we can't be in control of everything, and that's okay. Prayer is reaching out, which is something that's paramount to recovery in general. Prayer is the act of asking for help from a being or an understood greater influence over the universe. It's also a personal, one-on-one dialogue between ourselves and our higher power which can reveal some surprising things to us regarding what we ask for help with.

Prayer can also help us reconnect with people after treatment destroys our old network. That doesn't cast treatment into a very good light but think about the people in your life while substance use was or is part of it. How many of them have substance use or substance appropriation in common? If you haven't thought about your network in this light before, the answers might surprise you. The people that have drifted away might. Treatment seeks to cut your ties to that life and those triggers which can make you feel a little alone. Prayer can help you find the courage to restore bonds that were damaged or broken from addiction's hostile takeover and build a better outer support network from which to draw strength.

What is this higher power we've spoken about and to which we pray? Well, that's up to you. I can tell you that it'll be a little different for everyone in the same way that recovery is.

Think of a higher power as something greater than yourself and that you believe has control of the universe. If you're familiar with religion, this is the idea that God embodies, but that doesn't have to be your higher power. The most important part of your higher power is that it has meaning to you. It could be the universe, some manifestation of the universe, nature, or group consciousness. Belief in a higher power can help you turn your thoughts toward staying sober.

How does a belief do that? In three pretty specific ways. First, you learn to let things like pain and guilt go. You can turn it over to your higher power which allows for forgiveness and change because you've made space for it.

Second, it's a reassurance that you're not alone. You have your higher power in your corner as you face treatment, recovery, and the problems of addiction or life. Knowing you're not alone in the fight offers you a new kind of strength to push forward in your recovery and goals.

Third, a higher power can offer a new purpose to your life by opening up a new spiritual path. This path can gain the focus that addiction used to have, and the less attention substance use gets, the less likely it is to factor in your future. That's not to say that you forget about it. It's a disease, and management is important, but taking your primary focus from it and putting your focus on your new path might open up some surprising doors through which to help others and yourself.

That higher power sounds good. How do we find it? Start simple and talk with someone or a couple of people about what's important to you. Think like a well and be deep. What do you care about? The ocean? The natural world around you? The spirit within you and how you've always known that it's connected to something more than you?

All these things can lead you to contemplate that inexplicable force behind the universe. Whether it's your first trek down this path or a return to beliefs you lost during the worst of your addiction, it needs to be understood as something with greater power and control than you have. Don't worry if you can't quite put a name on it. That's common, and eventually, as your grasp of your higher power evolves, a name will follow. Moreover, a deeper understanding of your higher power will give you peace of mind and happiness.

Meditation helps us look within. The act of meditating has a physical reaction in the parietal lobe of our brains and actually slows its activity. This is the area where cravings manifest, and by slowing this part down, the rest of your brain catches up. It's like a brain reboot where damaged or blocked circuits are slowly rewired so that all sections of your brain can communicate in more effective patterns. As meditation opens up the management tools in your brain, you can find new ways to mitigate your cravings and even reduce their intensity.

Meditation reinvigorates your internal support network, but like all good things, it won't happen quickly. In terms of meditation and sticking with the reboot analogy, keep in mind that your brain is akin to a supercomputer. It stores a lot of information, has millions of networked pathways, and has a complex processing system. A full reboot takes time, energy, and work.

It might be difficult to find that quiet, centered place that allows you to focus. Lighting a candle and keeping your attention on it can be helpful for those new to meditation. The thing to remember is to be gentle with your brain. It's been on overload for a while, so when your thoughts wander, nudge them the way you'd nudge a leaf back into the flow of a current, and you'll find that calm, quiet internal place becomes easier to reach. This helps your brain manage those cravings and those trenches in a more efficient manner.

It's time to introduce our higher self. This is a term often associated with yoga, meditation, and other spiritual paths, but for our purposes, we'll define the higher self as the rational mind. This is the observer mind that lives within you and takes a more logical stance on situations and outcomes.

The higher self is the opposite of the ego self. The ego self is self-serving, keyed for survival, and it's the ego self where addiction lives and thrives or where we've lived in addiction. The ego self is all about short-term gratification and doesn't know how to navigate relationships.

Our higher self is interested in connecting to the good. This isn't necessarily a good versus evil idea but rather an ideal of what is inherently good. This can be the good that resides in God, the universe, or our higher power. The work that goes into transformation is to connect to the higher self so you can gain clarity and begin to think, feel, and behave in a way that's in tune with the higher self or the good that you feel resides within your higher power.

SPIRITUAL PRINCIPLES

The spiritual side of the 12 steps doesn't have a rulebook in the defined sense. Instead, spirituality is defined as universal truths. This is a similar idea to the good we seek through our higher self and higher power. Defining the guiding principles of spirituality isn't set in stone. There are thousands of iterations of the 12 step principles. For an idea to be spiritual, it needs to move you toward inner peace, contentedness, and happiness. They center on inclusion, oneness, and service to others and our community.

So, what I'm going to do is give you a list of spiritual principles that can be utilized as often in daily life as in the program. The most important things to remember when approaching the spiritual side of the program is to keep an open mind, retain your willingness to learn, and be honest, especially with yourself.

- Honesty is an integral part of step one.
- Hope is an integral part of step two.
- Faith is an important part of step three.
- Courage is an important part of step four.
- Integrity is an integral part of step five.
- Willingness is an integral part of recovery in general, step six in particular.
- Humility is an ongoing message and an integral part of step seven.

- Self-Discipline and discipline are integral parts of step eight.
- Forgiveness is an important part of step nine.
- Acceptance is an important part of recovery and also step ten.
- Spiritual awareness is an important concept of step eleven.
- Service is the defining point of step twelve.

Working the steps often entails living by principles, and there are far more than the ones listed in concurrence with each step. Each step has additional underlying principles which can be applied as they're worked. A great article by Dr. Howard Samuels (2013) details a similar type of list but goes one step further by applying them to life.

Faith, courage, forgiveness, acceptance, gratitude, and service are all part of Dr. Samuels' list. It's these kinds of principles that can change the way that we view ourselves and the world around us if we apply them with willingness and vigilance. Some of the additional principles may seem like common sense until we try to apply them consciously, but that doesn't mean we shouldn't try.

The ability to laugh at yourself, live in the moment, restraint of expression, remain teachable, and "everything you're looking for is already with you," make the list of truths. Remaining teachable is closely related to willingness and adds openness to new ideas and experiences from which to learn and grow.

The restraint notion closely relates to the idea of discipline and self-discipline. Restraint, in this conception, means asking if something needs to be said, if it needs to be said now, and if you really need to be the one to say it. This boils down to problem management; if you pause to ask these questions, the answers will likely be no. So, if you don't say it, you're not trying to micromanage, and you'll notice that some of those problems work themselves out. This one will probably take some finesse to get right, but that's where the vigilance aspect comes in.

We've touched on the idea of living in the moment, not dwelling in the past or obsessing over the future. The final two principles are laughing at yourself and "everything you're looking for." Maintaining your ability to laugh at yourself seems like a simple idea until someone you care for tells an embarrassing story about you or has a chuckle when you forget to zip your fly. Instead of running around with hurt feelings, recognize that embarrassing situations happen to everyone, so when you laugh at your embarrassment, you're creating a non-judgmental space for others to share in and laugh as well.

Next is the idea that everything you've been looking for, you brought with you. We've all spent time trying to find some way or something to fix us. This idea is closely tied to the ideas of self-love and forgiveness. One of the major ideas in the 12 step program and meditation is to look within. The reason is that our perfect inner self is right there, waiting to be discovered. This doesn't mean there aren't aspects that need work or change. It means that when we learn to discover, accept and love ourselves, we'll be able to connect with family, people, and our higher power in ways we couldn't imagine before.

SPIRITUAL AWAKENING

For some, this might sound a little like a B or made-for-TV movie script when you first read it, but that's our knee-jerk association of spiritualism and religions talking. Remember that the spiritual aspect of the program isn't necessarily tied to any religion at all. In this case, the idea of awakening becomes an "aha" moment. This is the moment words like "eureka" are made for. Does that mean it happens to everyone or all at once? No and no. Some go through life in recovery without ever having a moment that could be termed awakening. This doesn't mean that nothing happened. Everyone's recovery is different.

So, what is a spiritual awakening? It is a moment when we recognize a change without or within ourselves. It's a shift in our perspective that can come about in a variety of ways. It could make us a little uneasy, waiting for that moment, but not to worry. Even if you can't quite place the moment or the feeling, there are some simple ways to recognize your awakening moment.

This may be the moment when we look back on a situation and wonder why we handled it that way when now, we'd act differently. Maybe you've left behind your bitterness and regret and see, instead, why things happened, the beauty in it, and the lessons learned from it. You could notice that you pay more attention to how you think about others instead of worrying about how they think or perceive you. You begin to see and question the beauty and magic all around you.

Maybe you laugh and play more. It's become easier to recover from disappointments, so your moments of happiness happen more frequently. You honor your heart, bad habits slip away, and you're capable of unconditional love. Newfound freedom and purpose, clarity and intuition, or service, have replaced attachment and have become the dominant aspects of your life and your heart, and you're enjoying every minute of being right where you are.

Any of these things signal a spiritual awakening and what they have in common is what they lack. You've minimized your insecurities and fears, which means that you've left behind being the victim, acting in a self-seeking manner, and released your helplessness. You've learned, integrated your tools, and let go of condemnation, anger, and judgment of yourself and others.

We've been through the darkness, and now we are beginning to see the light and connect with a power greater than ourselves. If you want to dive deeper into spiritual awakening, please check out my other book, From the Universe with Love.

Affirmations

- I listen to the silence and receive answers from my higher power.
- I am opening my heart and my mind to a higher power.

7

HEALTHY CHOICES

It's like learning to ride a bike, you know? You have to get your bearings and you have to stay stable.

— EDIE FALCO

Healthy choices are something that might take us a little while to learn and understand. This ranks right up there with self-care and relearning how to get back into hygienic and healthy routines. Still no dancing, though, unless you choose to join a dance class to get your exercise. Then you'll learn a different kind of routine.

The types of choices we need to make start when our day does. Sleep is a very important part of having a good,

productive day and is an indispensable factor in our motivation. Often, the challenges of our life of addiction and the
following time spent in detox destroy our circadian rhythm,
which is our body's natural clock. To help our bodies get
back in rhythm, we can establish a simple routine that
signals our brains to wake up or wind down, depending on
the time of day.

It's as simple as making your bed. So, let's take a look at that
bed. If it's been more than seven years since you've gotten a
new one, you're probably due. In the bedroom and for our
quality of sleep, comfort is king. If you can't replace it right
away, set that as a goal. As long as it stays near the top of
your list, you'll get it and have your new routine set up for it.

This routine establishes a simple type of motivation that
carries over into the rest of your day. When you get up in the
morning, make your bed, and you've accomplished your first
task. Then open your curtains. A face full of sunshine helps
your brain understand that it's morning and time to get
started.

At bedtime, reverse your routine. Close your curtains, which
signals to your brain that it's time to wind down and pull
down the covers. If you find that you're having a difficult
time getting entirely relaxed, check for things like blue light
or your nightlight. If your nightlight is at eye level, it's
tricking your brain into thinking that you need to stay
awake. It's recommended to shut off electronics thirty

minutes before bed since blue light engages different sections of the brain. This would be a perfect time to relax and read.

Another healthy choice you can make is to get into nature. Time spent connecting to nature and animals and listening to natural sounds has been proven to reduce the level of cortisol in the brain. Cortisol is a stress-inducing chemical, so less cortisol means more relaxation and less anxiety or depression.

Working nature into your day is as simple as taking a walk or having lunch at the park. If you're in a concrete jungle, seek out the trees planted in garden areas or along roads, and spend a little time with them. The sound of the wind through the leaves and birds perched in the branches are waiting to serenade you.

If you'd rather take a more active role, volunteering at a local nature park, preserve, or trail is a way to both be of service and engage with the natural wonders of the world. Starting or getting involved in a personal or community garden is another option and offers the added bonus of watching things grow and blossom.

Take a daily walk through your neighborhood. During these walks, pay attention to how things change as the seasons progress. You'll find buds and early flowers in the spring, the full splendor of canopies and gardens in the summer, and the new colors as autumn creeps in. In the winter, you might find an evergreen or everbearing bush hidden away and peppered with berries.

Meditating for ten minutes on the beach or out in the sun is another way to engage and soak in the wonders of nature. It might become your favorite way to focus and practice mindfulness. You can bring nature inside with you and play a radio station or TV channel dedicated to nature sounds. The sounds of water are proven to help relaxation in various forms.

Finding new kinds of fun has come up a few times, but we've barely scratched the surface of things you can do. One of the ways we can discover fun is to seek out a different kind of excitement through outdoor sports or activities. Things like intramural sports, kayaking, or skiing are both challenging and exciting from the first.

Try exercise. The most basic exercise has been proven to support resolve and certainty in recovery. It's also a great way to destress, stay occupied, improve how you feel about yourself, and improve your rest. The chemicals released in the brain during exercise-also called a runner's high-are mood-lifting endorphins, among others. The best part is you don't have to go to the gym. You can try yoga which improves core strength and helps us focus on mindfulness through meditation.

Exploring our interests or reawakening past interests that we gave up is another way to have fun. Search for workshops or classes in your area or online which cater to your interests. This feeds into the idea of finding hobbies that interest you. A cooking class might awaken a new love for French cuisine, or a pottery class might unlock a hidden talent for sculpture.

You could get a dog. Caring for a pet is both a responsibility and a hobby. They require training, but there are some added benefits to having a puppy. They act as added support during your recovery and offer comfort. It's also been proven that time spent with a dog lowers cortisol levels in your brain which means you're less stressed and anxious. You might make some interesting new friends through your four-legged companion as well.

Planning activities with family or friends can have the added bonus of helping to repair damaged relationships. Doing things like dinners, attending plays, or trips to the movies are all ways to reconnect to yourself and those you love. You could throw a sober party. Planning it will keep you busy, and as long as you stick to the sober rule, you can let the good times roll with games, fright night features, and other themes.

If you'd rather get out and do things, you could enhance your meditation skills with a yoga class. Volunteering is another way to fill time, give back, and uncover waiting interests. If there's a sober bar in your area, you can go to it and socialize with fruity drinks minus the drug.

Affirmations

- I live with purpose today.
- I do the next right thing when no one is looking.

8

CHANGE YOUR THOUGHTS,
CHANGE YOUR WORLD

Life is very interesting... in the end, some of your greatest pains become your greatest strengths.

— DREW BARRYMORE

We're going to dive into a different kind of change and level up your self-talk. The way that we see the world is a mixed bag of experiences and beliefs tinted by our lenses as it enters into our central processing unit (a.k.a. our brains), and like your favorite device, our brains have certain filters and settings established. In order to change and level up, we need to update our internal settings and filters.

Our recovery journey is about working on ourselves so that we can manage our disease in the most effective ways for us. One of the things we need to consider is our mindset. Do we have a stagnant or growth outlook?

A stagnant outlook is one that doesn't allow for change, particularly with ourselves, but also with everything in general. The world is how it is, people are how they are, and they're not going to get better or worse. It's like unmoving, locked-up water that gathers bacteria and sits in its bank, doing nothing and going nowhere.

A growth mindset invites change, not only for yourself but for the people and world around you. It's more like that river we keep returning to because it allows for flow and shifts naturally. Flow leads to change and a greater understanding of what's happening in our internal and external worlds. It stays fresh and vibrant because it's always flowing somewhere.

Why so serious about this one? It's not an easy thing to approach the way that we think about things. For this change, we need a judgment-free, safe zone attitude and to have honesty with ourselves. Many of us might have established a habit of being too hard on ourselves, but this isn't conducive to a growth mindset. There's a difference between taking responsibility and beating ourselves up.

The first step is to work on our filters by unlearning the habits and patterns that got us into this situation. This begins when we start our recovery journey, and we need to foster awareness of that idea. Some of those patterns, such as our thought patterns, might take a little time and regard to change toward growth.

The second step is learning where to reset those filters so that they become more productive, helpful tools. When we reset our filters to allow for change, we can level up our self-talk, and that has the potential to change everything. We are essentially giving ourselves permission to become the best version of ourselves that we can be despite the chronic condition we're managing.

So, we know that there will be setbacks and maybe we'll slip or stumble. Maybe a step gives us a little trouble, and we feel like giving up. Maybe we're starting to wonder why we thought recovery was a good idea. Think honestly about what you're really giving up. Not the rose-tinted memories but the other stuff that might make you cringe and shake your head. Now, let's remind ourselves why we chose this road and focus on the reason that brought us into treatment or to a program. Whether it's your spouse, parents, kids, career, or health, our personal reason for undertaking this road is our cornerstone. If you compare what you're giving up to your cornerstone and what you want to keep or gain, recovery is more than worth the work. That's filter one.

Filter two is giving yourself a break. When you stumble, have trouble, or can't seem to summit that mountain, don't beat yourself up. Negativity won't get you closer to your goals. Instead, give "yet" the power. Say, "I'm not ready for that yet." By adding the word yet, we're giving ourselves time for growth, space to return, and permission to try until we succeed. When we use "yet," we can change our mindset toward setting and achieving goals. As long as you're being mindful and actively trying, you're on the right road.

The next filter we need to update is the tone of our self-talk. We've discussed using the just for today card as a guide and giving focus to self-care. The more positive our self-talk and pep talks are, the more resilience we can muster. Be mindful of your doubts and when they start up, give yourself a pep talk. It works for more than cravings and can be as simple as a reminder of an accomplishment or positive change you've already made. "I did that, so I can do this, too."

Our fourth filter is to allow more self-validation. Too often, we strive to reach goals for others' approval, and when we do, we're not being true to ourselves. When we're true to who we are, we allow ourselves to be authentic. If we allow ourselves to be satisfied by what we accomplish, we can add that to our self-talk and grow into the person we want to be.

Next, we need to allow ourselves the grace to learn from our mistakes. These encompass those from way back when and those that are around the corner. Instead of spending hours picking apart everything you did wrong, ask yourself how you can do things differently the next time. Challenge yourself to find what you learned from doing things that way, be it about yourself, the situation, or life in general. Learning from experience is a positive way to help yourself embrace a growth mindset.

Finally, we need to transform jealousy, be it of a mentor, another program member, or the guy next door. Everyone has setbacks, and everyone travels their own road. Instead of envying what you think someone's doing or what they have, turn it into inspiration. If you see Joe doing something or living his best life and it's something that you want, set it as a goal. Utilize your support system and sponsor as mentors that inspire you to be the best version of yourself and expand your possibilities.

Making these changes can be accomplished in a few different ways. You can connect with others through volunteering or fellowship with those in your home group. Give your family members a call. Connecting with others, whether in big or small ways, opens our minds up to other ways of thinking outside ourselves.

Giving back through volunteer work exposes us to others' situations and gives us the opportunity to help someone else. Lending an ear or shoulder to a friend in need can do the same. Giving positivity will often foster it in our lives as well.

Exercising ticks off one of the self care boxes and gives us all the benefits that go with it, including better mental acuity, physical health, and sleep. We can add to our self care and our growth by giving ourselves time and learning to accept. Allow yourself the time it takes you in recovery. As long as you're working the steps at your pace, you're doing it the right way. The thing that can derail us is complacency, but complacency can't exist if you're working the steps and being mindful. It's your journey, so it's your pace. There's no need to rush and accumulate stress.

Accepting situations, however difficult, gives you the chance to learn and grow from them. Sometimes difficulties happen, and all that we can control is our perspective of it. That's where acceptance plays a role, and the more acceptance and forgiveness we have for ourselves, the more that we're able to control our reaction and perspective in difficulties.

"I AM"

This is the final filter. The words "I am" begin most of our self-talk. We learn to criticize ourselves, and we're conditioned along the course of our lives into "I am not." If we fail a test or quiz, our reaction is, "I'm not smart." If a loved one leaves us, our reaction is, "I am not worth it, worthy, or lovable."

In truth, these constructs have no place in our internal world. In the external, real world, where things are measured and where input is defined by our senses, there are boundaries to everything.

Consider your higher power and all the things in its control. If it's truly the connection to our spirit, then our spirit is as free of external constructs as our higher power. "I am not" is like putting in a firewall. Firewalls serve their purpose, but this is one of those places they can produce negative self-talk instead of positive. When we change our outlook from "I am not" to "I am," we remove the constructs from our higher power and allow change within.

So, changing this filter is like giving our spirit full contact with our higher power. Instead of using the filters of the external world, "I am" allows the internal world to be what it was meant to be. We remove this filter one "I am not" situation at a time. When our loved one chooses to end a relationship, instead of saying "I'm not worthy," say, "I am love." When applying for that promotion, our mindset shifts from "I'm not capable of" or "I hope to have" to "I am capable" and "I am going to have."

By making this change, we're giving our trust to our spirit, our higher self, or our higher power. We're inviting the idea that we can be or do what we want and reframing our self-concept into a positive outlook.

AFFIRMATIONS

At the end of each chapter, you might have noticed affirmations. This is because another way to update our settings is to add affirmations into our self-talk. Affirmations are more than quirky, motivational slogans, and people from many walks of life have begun to utilize the power of affirmations in their daily lives. There's some science to this trend and the positivity it fosters.

One of the ideas in counseling and therapy is to change your view of yourself to improve your mental health. The idea is that the way that we see ourselves is flexible and that we can choose to see ourselves as capable or smart through self-affirmation. Through this idea, we can introduce our brain to new concepts, which, in turn, creates new pathways of thought and reasoning.

Think about this. If Joe is constantly saying, "I am old," then Joe's mind will set that concept as its running system. However, if Joe says, "I am teachable," he's opened up that part of his brain to learning from any situation he finds himself in. His age, whether actual or psychological, factors in less because he's allowing himself to be teachable.

The structure of affirmations allows us to gain a more optimistic outlook and reduces the amount of cortisol and other stress hormones. It activates the prefrontal cortex, and the more that we repeat the affirmations, the more that we engage that area of the brain, which reinforces our positive mindset. Affirmations can help us lead healthier lifestyles and reduce our chances of stress-induced health problems.

The trick to affirmations is that you must allow yourself to **believe in it, feel it on every level, and have faith in it.** Use your new power of "I am" and add affirmations to bring your positive self-talk to the next level.

Affirmations

- I am worthy of love and happiness.
- I am enough.

CONCLUSION

Recovery is the road that we choose. It's different for everyone, and at times, it's difficult for everyone. My journey includes seven months of treatment. My drug of choice is alcohol, and the group that works for me is NA. If recovery doesn't stick the first time, keep coming back. Relapse happens, life happens, and people aren't perfect. The key is to continue to work on ourselves. We might be powerless over our disease, but we have the power to pursue recovery.

Just like Joe with Parkinson's, it takes work to make a change. We didn't ask for a chronic illness, but the longer our illness goes untreated, the more we miss out on, and the more destruction it causes in our lives, both externally and internally. Taking responsibility for our recovery is the greatest tool in our kit. When we accept responsibility, we can maneuver through the five steps.

Through the five steps and recovery, we can begin the journey into a better version of ourselves. The first part of that journey is admission. The second step is asking for help, be it through a treatment program or by finding and attending your first 12 step meeting. All we need to bring to either of those things is an open mind and a willingness to accept change one day at a time. It's available, and recovery works. We crunched the numbers and laid out the facts to prove it.

When we're on the journey, working the steps is paramount. If we get that thirst or that craving, remember our exit strategy and have our safety plan ready. Use society's distractions to your advantage to manage your cravings and mitigate your triggers. Engage in sober fun and fellowship, give your sponsor a call, or take a walk with a trusted friend. There's a phone with you so you can handle high-risk situations. There's a bathroom somewhere close by to take a breath, have a moment, and try again.

Play the Tape through. The haze of euphoria is a game played by our tricky minds because the brain seeks out the paths it knows. So push it back onto the recovery path and remind yourself why you chose recovery. Remember the drama and ocean of regret that happened or the way that you hit bottom. Play the Tape as if life depends on it because our sobriety surely does.

Use your gratitude journal every day, and you'll find all the moments when happiness happens. Change is right around the corner, and a spiritual awakening might occur when you least expect it. And remember to pack a little away for a rainy day but don't worry about the flood until it starts raining. That way, we can breathe deep in the sunshine.

Have a piece of gum when anxiety threatens to trick your brain into a more relaxed state and logical frame. Be vigilant for the warning stages of relapse, as well. Remember, there's more to it than the physical act. Our mental and emotional state have their own warning signs. 90 in 90 works for more than forming the habit of going to a meeting, and if those warning signs crop up, renew the habit. Let's enjoy our home group, invest in our recovery, and be mindful of our routine, self-care, and spiritual life.

Staying responsible gives us access to the other heavy hitters in our kit—things like forgiveness that can spawn a world of change. Things like acceptance and prayer connect us to something greater than ourselves; however, you define it. Responsibility gives us access to reboot our supercomputer, so it engages more than the same old paths. From there, we can update and reset our filters, engage our positive mindset, and give ourselves the leveled-up pep talks we never knew we needed.

All these things, the steps, and the literature available to add to our day can fill the time we spent finding and using our substance of choice. It doesn't matter what predisposition led to our disease. What matters is that addiction only cares that we're people. We might not have the same backgrounds, triggers, addictions, or recovery, but we all struggle with the same disease.

Fill your time by volunteering. You have more than you think, even if it's just a few minutes earlier to a meeting than normal or folding clothes at a clothing drive. Take a visit to a shelter, help in the community garden, or call your friends to help with a food drive.

Now, go out and play a game, take a walk, or hug your dog. Do the next right thing and engage with your higher self. Find a hobby that makes you smile. Better, find one that makes you laugh, whether at yourself or out of the joy of being in the moment. There will be tough times down the road, but your toolkit is ready and waiting. It's big, and it packs a punch. You're not stuck with a blender in a river any longer.

Included after this are links to national hotlines to begin your journey. **If you found the five steps helpful, please tell others who might benefit from what we've learned, and if you don't mind, kindly leave a review on Amazon.** After all, we can't keep what we have without giving it away.

ADDITIONAL RESOURCES

Substance Abuse and Addiction Hotline
https://drughelpline.org/

Drug Abuse Hotline
https://www.help.org/drug-abuse-hotline/

Go to www.bellemotley.com
scan the QR code for your free gift

A Free Gift for You!

In the "Vibe Guide," you will learn...

- **15 techniques** to raise your vibrations and
stay in a high frequency

- How to manifest your desires

- How to find peace...

and so much more!

REFERENCES

A guide to navigating high-risk situations in recovery. (n.d.). ALYST Health. https://www.alysthealth.com/navigating-high-risk-situations-in-recovery/

Adams, M. (2017, September 28). *What percentage of addicts stay clean?* Whitesands Treatment. https://whitesandstreatment.com/2017/09/28/what-percentage-of-addicts-stay-clean/

Adams, M. (2020, December 2). *Famous celebrity quotes about addiction and recovery*. Whitesands Treatment. https://whitesandstreatment.com/2020/12/02/10-quotes-from-celebrities-who-have-beaten-addiction/

Addictions Content Team. (2021, September 16). *The addiction treatment FAQ*. Addictions.com. https://www.addictions.com/faq/

AlcoholRehab.com. (n.d.). *Blame and addiction*. https://alcoholrehab.com/alcohol-recovery/blame-and-addiction/

AlcoholRehab.com. (n.d.). *One day at a time in recovery*. https://alcoholrehab.com/alcohol-recovery/aftercare/one-day-at-a-time/

Allard, A. (2019, February 27). *Putting our recovery first—Defenders of sobriety*. Defenders of Sobriety. http://defendersofsobriety.org/putting-our-recovery-first/

American Addiction Centers (n.d.). *12 step programs: 12 steps to recovery for addiction*. https://americanaddictioncenters.org/rehab-guide/12-step

Andy. (2021, November 9). *How to change your mindset about addiction recovery*. Calm. https://calmrehab.com/how-to-change-your-mindset-about-addiction-recovery/

Blais, S. (2017, December 10). *You can't keep it unless you give it away*. Thought Catalog. https://thoughtcatalog.com/seth-blais/2017/12/you-cant-keep-it-unless-you-give-it-away/

Blakeney, Y. (2021, June 7). *Understanding the higher self*. Recover Integrity. https://www.recoverintegrity.com/2021/06/07/understanding-high-self/

Castan, R. (2020, April 22). *Changing your mindset in addiction recovery*. Spring-Board Recovery. https://www.springboardrecovery.com/changing-your-mindset-in-addiction-recovery/

Close, L. (n.d.). *Drug & alcohol addiction among socioeconomic groups.* Sunrise House. https://sunrisehouse.com/addiction-demographics/socioeconomic-groups/

Common relapse triggers and how to avoid them. (2019, December 13). Gateway Foundation. https://www.gatewayfoundation.org/addiction-blog/triggers-in-addiction-recovery/

Corbitt, S. (2021, June 28). *The science behind the power of affirmations.* Create Your Happy. https://createyourhappy.org/the-science-behind-the-power-of-affirmations/

Cory, P. (2022, February 25). *Why are prayer and meditation suggested as tools of recovery?* Essentials Recovery. https://www.essentialsrecovery.com/why-are-prayer-and-meditation-suggested-as-tools-of-recovery/

Derry, J. & Derry, J. (2022, June 1). *Gratitude in recovery.* Medium.https://medium.com/recovery-freedom-from-addiction/gratitude-in-recovery-e232b9962ba5

Derry, J. & Derry, J. (2022, July 7). *Play the tape through.* Medium https://medium.com/recovery-freedom-from-addiction/play-the-tape-through-80ddddf592c3

Doub, T. W. (n.d.). *Disease of addiction.* American Addiction Centers. https://americanaddictioncenters.org/disease-of-addiction

Drug abuse hotline. (n.d.). Help.org. https://www.help.org/drug-abuse-hotline/

Dyer, W. W. (2012, November 7). *The power of I am.* Dr. Wayne W Dyer. https://www.drwaynedyer.com/blog/the-power-of-i-am/

Ellis, M. E. (2021, October 7). *The power of gratitude in your recovery.* Alta Mira Recovery. https://www.altamirarecovery.com/blog/the-power-of-gratitude-in-your-recovery/

F, C. (2018, September 16). *The dangers of complacency in sobriety.* Find Addiction Rehabs. https://findaddictionrehabs.com/dangers-complacency-in-sobriety/

Forgiving yourself: Releasing regrets in addiction recovery. (2019, November 29). The Hills Treatment Center. https://thehillscenter.com/addiction-blog/addiction-recovery-and-forgiveness/

How a positive mindset can make a difference in addiction recovery. (2021, August 29). Casa Palmera. https://casapalmera.com/blog/positive-mindset-addiction-recovery/

How to naturally recover from addiction (Without Treatment). (2021, May 6). The

Walker   Center.   https://www.thewalkercenter.org/blog-posts/how-to-naturally-recover-from-addiction-without-treatment

Inspirational quotes from famous people in recovery.(n.d.). American Behavioral Clinics.   https://americanbehavioralclinics.com/inspirational-quotes-from-famous-people-in-recovery/

Intro: spiritual principles behind the 12 steps of AA. (2021, April 13). Spirit Centered Sober Living. https://spiritcentersoberliving.com/recovery/spiritual-principles/intro-spiritual-principles-12-steps-of-aa/

Is reading important in the addiction recovery process. (n.d.). Cypress Lakes Lodge. https://www.cypresslakeslodge.com/the-importance-of-reading-in-addiction-recovery/

Jessup, M. A., Ross, T. B., Jones, A. L., Satre, D. D., Weisner, C. M., Chi, F. W., & Mertens, J. R. (2014). Significant life events and their impact on alcohol and drug use: A qualitative study. *Journal of Psychoactive Drugs*, 46(5), 450–459. https://doi.org/10.1080/02791072.2014.962715

Koulouris, C. (2019, September 23). *How to have fun in addiction recovery: Finding activities addressing bad habits.* Scallywag and Vagabond. https://scallywagandvagabond.com/2019/09/having-fun-addiction-recovery-activities/

Kunst, J. (2016, November 29). *12 promises and 12 rewards.* Amethyst Recovery Center. https://www.amethystrecovery.org/12-promises-12-rewards/

Legacy Healing Center. (2020, October 30). *Celebrity quotes on addiction and recovery.*   https://www.legacyhealing.com/10-quotes-from-celebrities-who-have-recovered-from-drug-and-alcohol-addiction/

Literature and other products. (n.d.). Narcotics Anonymous. https://www.na.org/?ID=literature

Mental health and addiction: Benefits of having a positive mindset. (2021, December 15). Haven House. Addiction Recovery for Men. https://havenhouserecovery.com/mental-health-and-addiction-benefits-of-having-a-positive-mindset/

Merrill, J. (n.d.). *Substance abuse & addiction hotline.* National Drug Helpline. https://drughelpline.org/

Murphy, E. (n.d.). *Addiction and genetics.* Recovered. https://recovered.org/addiction/addiction-and-genetics

NA World Services. (2022). *Recovery products NAWS web store canada.* https://cart-ca.na.org/recovery-products/?page=1

Narcotics Anonymous World Services, Inc. (1986). *NA white booklet.* https://na.org/admin/include/spaw2/uploads/pdf/litfiles/us_english/Booklet/NA%20White%20Booklet.pdf

Narcotics Anonymous World Services, Inc. (1986). *What is the narcotics anonymous program?* https://www.na.org/admin/include/spaw2/uploads/pdf/litfiles/us_english/misc/What%20Is%20the%20NA%20Program.pdf

Narcotics Anonymous World Services, Inc. (1986). *How it works.* https://na.org/admin/include/spaw2/uploads/pdf/litfiles/us_english/misc/How%20it%20Works.pdf

Nicosia, D. (2021, September 21). *Benefits of sobriety: Seven great things that happen to you when you stop using drugs or alcohol.* Recovery Unplugged. https://www.recoveryunplugged.com/benefits-of-sobriety-seven-great-things-that-happen-to-you-when-you-stop-using-drugs-or-alcohol/

Oregon Trail Recovery. (2021, March 31). *Different types of 12 step meetings (NA, AA, CMA, etc.).* https://oregontrailrecovery.com/blog/types-of-12-step-meetings/

Parental Alienation Anonymous. (2021, August 10). *What is a 12 step meeting? (common questions).* https://parentalalienationanonymous.com/what-is-a-12-step-meeting-common-questions/

Paul. (2020, January 31). *The importance of a higher power in recovery.* Silver Maple Recovery. https://www.silvermaplerecovery.com/blog/higher-power-recovery/

Raypole, C. (2020, May 28). *Everything you need to know about psychological dependence.* Healthline. https://www.healthline.com/health/psychological-addiction

Recovery from addiction glossary. (n.d.). Recovery Connection. https://www.recoveryconnection.com/glossaries/recovery/

Renascent. (2016, December 16). *A step 12 guide: Spiritual awakenings in addiction Recovery.* https://renascent.ca/step-12-guide-spiritual-awakenings-addiction-recovery/

Restoration and Recovery Center. (2021, November 3). *The role of nature in addiction recovery.* https://restorationrecoverycenter.com/the-role-of-nature-in-addiction-recovery/

Risk of complacency in recovery. (n.d.). Addiction Helpline. https://www.addiction.org.uk/risk-of-complacency-in-recovery/

Samuels, H. C. (2013, November 10). *Emotional sobriety in recovery: 12 spiritual principles to live by*. Addiction Blog. https://alcohol.addictionblog.org/ emotional-sobriety-in-recovery-12-spiritual-principles-to-live-by/

Sober Recovery. (2006, April 28). *Guidelines for male sponsor/female sponsee.* https://www.soberrecovery.com/forums/narcotics-addiction-12-step-support/92844-guidelines-male-sponsor-female-sponsee.html

Spero Recovery. (2022, June 25). *How to create an effective safety plan.* https:// www.sperorecovery.org/how-to-create-an-effective-safety-plan/

Spiritual growth in addiction recovery. (2019, May 16). Royal Life Centers. https://royallifecenters.com/spiritual-growth-in-addiction-recovery/

Stoddart, T. (2011, December 20). *Taking suggestions.* Sober Nation. https:// sobernation.com/taking-suggestions/

Stop playing the addiction blame game. (2014, August 27). Promises Behavioral Health. https://www.promises.com/addiction-blog/stop-playing-addiction-blame-game/

T, B. (n.d.). *A study of step 12 of the 12-step programs.* Verywell Mind. https:// www.verywellmind.com/a-study-of-step-12-69412

The importance of service in recovery. (2019, January 6). A Better Today Recovery Services. https://www.abtrs.com/news/the-importance-of-service-in-recovery

The power of gratitude in addiction recovery. (2016, May 24). The Cabin Chiang Mai. https://www.thecabinchiangmai.com/blog/the-power-of-gratitude-in-addiction-recovery/

The Recovery Village. (n.d.). *Is it okay to date in early recovery? Dangers & tips for dating in recovery.* https://www.therecoveryvillage.com/recovery/ok-to-date-in-early-recovery/

Thrive. (2018, November 20). *Addiction is not your fault... But it is your responsibility.* Thrive Treatment. https://thrivetreatment.com/addiction-is-not-your-fault-but-it-is-your-responsibility/

Tranquil Shores. (2017, October 24). *How your environment affects addiction.* https://www.tranquilshores.org/blog/2017/october/how-your-environment-affects-addiction/

Trauma and addiction. (n.d.). Stages of Recovery. https://stagesrecoverycenters. com/trauma-and-addiction/

Twelve Steps to Recovery. (2021, March 18). *12 step literature: Guiding texts for twelve step recovery programmes.* https://www.12steps.nz/12-steps-programme/12-step-literature/

What is a spiritual awakening in recovery? (2022, April 1). Covenant Hills. https://covenanthillstreatment.com/spiritual-awakening in recovery/

What is a spiritual awakening in recovery? (n.d.). Safe & Sound Treatment. https://safesoundtreatment.com/what-is-a-spiritual-awakening-in-recovery/

What is self-care in addiction recovery and how do you practice it? (2021, September 8). Hannah's House. https://www.hannahshouse.com/what-is-self-care-in-addiction-recovery/

What it means to work the program. (n.d.). 12 Step.com. https://www.12step.com/articles/what-it-means-to-work-the-program

Why is a homegroup so important? (2020, July 4). Valiant Living Detox and Assessment. https://www.valiantdetox.com/why-is-a-homegroup-so-important/

Why making your bed can change your recovery routine. (2019, June 11). Oceanfront Recovery. https://www.oceanfrontrecovery.com/rehab-blog/why-making-your-bed-can-change-your-recovery-routine/

Why 90 meetings in 90 days? (n.d.). 12 Step.com. https://www.12step.com/articles/why-90-meetings-in-90-days

Printed in Great Britain
by Amazon